THE NUTS AND BOLTS OF REINSURANCE

BY

KEITH RILEY

|LLP|

LONDON   HONG KONG
1997

LLP Limited
Legal & Business Publishing Division
69–77 Paul Street
London EC2A 4LQ
Great Britain

SOUTH EAST ASIA
LLP Asia Limited
Room 1101, Hollywood Centre
233 Hollywood Road
Hong Kong

© Keith Riley, 1997

British Library Cataloguing in Publication Data
A catalogue record
for this book is available
from the British Library

ISBN 1–85978–106–3

All rights reserved. No part of this publication may be reproduced, stored in a retrieval system, or transmitted, in any form or by any means, electronic, mechanical, photocopying, recording or otherwise, without the prior written permission of LLP Limited.

Whilst every effort has been made to ensure that the information contained in this book is correct, neither the author nor LLP Limited can accept any responsibility for any errors or omissions or for any consequences arising therefrom.

Text set in 10/12pt Plantin by
Selwood Systems, Midsomer Norton
Printed in Great Britain by
WBC Ltd, Bridgend,
Mid-Glamorgan

ACKNOWLEDGEMENTS

To all the people whose help and encouragement have made this book possible, I extend my sincerest thanks. In particular, my wife Emma and son Matthew have tolerated my prolonged periods locked away at weekends. Grateful thanks are also due in rich measure to my friend and colleague, Edward Harrison, for his diligent proofreading of several manuscripts, and for his encouragement at times when my enthusiasm was flagging.

PREFACE

There have been several books written on the subject of reinsurance, so what is different about this one?

My purpose in writing this book is to simplify some of the concepts of reinsurance, as well as to record for posterity the more common technical matters which are becoming increasingly overlooked in a rapidly changing world.

The advent of the computer brought about some major changes in the daily routine of the reinsurance person, and many of the daily tasks of 20 years ago are omitted from the training regime of today.

These changes have been a necessary part of making our business more efficient, but I sometimes worry that the people who have joined the industry in the last 10 years are not acquiring some of the basic skills before being sent out into the world to advise insurance companies on their reinsurance requirements. Sooner or later, this lack of understanding of the rudiments of reinsurance will be exposed, and the reputation of the individual, and, indeed, of his company, will suffer as a result.

I do not condemn the use of computers. They take away the drudgery of the most routine tasks, and free the individual to pursue more creative activities, which may ultimately benefit his client. However, we should not allow the computer to prevent us from understanding the concepts involved in what we are doing, any more than the use of an electronic calculator should excuse us from learning the principles of long multiplication, the use of the slide rule, or how logarithms work. Quite simply, we should be able to do everything we ask our computers to do, albeit rather more slowly.

A very simple example of this is the spreadsheet. Using a simple spreadsheet, anybody could copy in a few figures and produce a beautiful set of statistics to present to an underwriter. But if the person preparing those statistics has no understanding of the relationship between the premiums, commissions, portfolio transfers, claims, loss ratios, etc., he cannot possibly be expected to notice some glaring errors in the figures. On the other hand, if he has the ability to prepare the same statistics manually, he is far more likely to spot such errors. Better still, if he has the ability to prepare the spreadsheet from scratch, using all of the mathematical formulae necessary to ensure the minimum amount of keying in of figures, he will be far better equipped to analyse statistical information, which is one of the key requirements of a modern reinsurance professional.

Where appropriate, I shall make reference to the ways in which personal computers can help us in our daily work, and I shall supplement this with a few of my own "recipes" which you may find useful, and may even be able to improve upon. However, the emphasis must be on understanding the processes involved.

December 1996   KEITH RILEY

ABOUT THE AUTHOR

Keith Riley started his career at Sedgwick Forbes in 1973. After spending four years in the Facultative Reinsurance Department, he was seconded to *Irano British Insurance Services* in Tehran for six months, where he was involved in direct insurance broking.

Upon returning to London in 1978 he worked on the Middle East Department of the Treaty Reinsurance Division. Since then he has also been involved with treaty reinsurance business in Latin America, Europe and the Far East. He is currently the Account Executive for the Middle East Treaty Department of Sedgwick Reinsurance Brokers, and has recenty delivered reinsurance workshops and seminars in Brazil and Japan.

TABLE OF CONTENTS

	Page
Acknowledgements	v
Preface	vii
About the author	ix

CHAPTER 1 WHAT IS REINSURANCE, AND WHY DO WE NEED IT? — 1

CHAPTER 2 TYPES OF REINSURANCE — 5

Facultative	5
Pro-rata (or proportional)	7
Excess of loss (non-proportional)	9
Treaties	13
Pro-rata Treaties	14
Quota Share Treaties	14
Surplus Treaties	15
Facultative Obligatory covers	17
Cessions to treaties	19
Special considerations	19
Basis of cession	19
Top Location and pro-rata basis	20
PML basis	20
Per policy basis	21
Per bottom basis	21
Per vessel basis	21
Per person basis	22
Practical Exercise 1—Distribution of Premiums and claims over a proportional programme	23

CHAPTER 3 TREATY REINSURANCE—FINANCIAL ASPECTS — 25

Premiums	26
Commission	27
Tax	28
Premium reserves	28
Loss reserves	29

xii Table of Contents

Interest on reserves	30
How reserves are accounted	31
Losses	32
Cash loss refunds	32
Premium and loss portfolio transfers	34
Underwriting Year basis	34
"Clean Cut" basis	35
Calculation of unexpired premiums	36
The 1/24ths system	37
1/8ths system	38
A fixed percentage	38
What if the Quota Share percentage changes?	39
What if a reinsurer's share changes?	39
What if treaty limits increase/reduce?	39
What if the treaty is cancelled?	40
How are portfolio transfers affected by premium and loss reserves?	40
Profit commission	40
Income	41
Practical Exercises 2(a) and (b)—profit commission calculations	43
Deficit carry forward	43
Underwriting year basis	44
What happens if we have a Quota Share Treaty, and the retention changes?	46
What happens if the shares of individual reinsurers change?	46
CHAPTER 4 PROPORTIONAL TREATY WORDINGS AND CLAUSES	**49**
Period and termination	49
Errors and Omissions	51
Self insured obligations	51
Inspection of records	51
Arbitration	52
Bordereaux	53
CHAPTER 5 DESIGNING A PROPERTY REINSURANCE PROGRAMME FROM HISTORICAL DATA	**55**
Data	58
Apportionment over the treaty programme	60
Constructing the spreadsheet	61
CHAPTER 6 EXCESS OF LOSS COVERS	**71**
Financial aspects	77
Premium	77
Rate	77
Premium income	78
(Minimum and) Deposit Premium	78
The "penal" M & D	79

Worked example	79
Other variable factors	80
Loss payments	80
"Hours Clause"	80
Practical Exercise 3—Allocating claims over an excess of loss programme	81
Reinstatement Premiums	83
Burning Cost rating	85
Working covers	86
Definition of Burning Cost	86
Burning Cost spreadsheet model	90

CHAPTER 7   EXCESS OF LOSS RATING   95

Exposure rating	95
1. The risk profile	96
2. First Loss Scale	97
3. Poisson Tables/Formula	98
Constructing the property risk excess rating model	98
Catastrophe rating	108
Constructing a catastrophe rating model	111

CHAPTER 8   MARKET EVOLUTION   115

CHAPTER 9   OVER TO YOU   117

Contact me   117

APPENDIX 1   ANSWERS TO PRACTICAL EXERCISE 1   119

APPENDIX 2   ANSWERS TO PRACTICAL EXERCISE 2   121

APPENDIX 3   ANSWERS TO PRACTICAL EXERCISE 3   125

APPENDIX 4   SPECIMEN SCALE OF PROPERTY FIRST LOSS RATES   127

APPENDIX 5   SPECIMEN TREATY WORDINGS   129

Non Marine Surplus Treaty	129
Motor and General Liability Excess of Loss	140
Marine Cargo and Hull Excess of Loss	155
General Catastrophe Excess of Loss	167

Index   177

CHAPTER 1

WHAT IS REINSURANCE, AND WHY DO WE NEED IT?

To answer this most basic question, we need to go back to the origins of insurance itself. By this, I do not mean all that stuff about Mr Lloyd's coffee shop or the merchants of Lombardy; enough has been written elsewhere on this. What we are talking about are the basic concepts, leaving out the historical detail. To do this, I shall rely on a short parable.

Fred Bloggs lived in a village, in a modest cottage. There were about a hundred similar cottages in Fred's village. One day, Fred's cottage burned to the ground, and Fred was left homeless and destitute. Fortunately, Fred had very good neighbours who clubbed together to rebuild Fred's cottage. They also collected some old furniture, so that he had somewhere to sit, to eat from and to sleep.

The moral of the story is that one man's loss was shared among a hundred people, and each of them could manage their share of the burden. This is insurance in its most basic form.

Now, as life became more complex, and good neighbours harder to find, the village co-operative approach to insuring risk became unreliable. Try knocking on your neighbours' doors after your house burns down and see if their good neighbourliness extends to helping you replace your house and possessions.

Very soon, the professionals moved in. Lloyd's underwriters were among the first (but not necessarily where insuring homes is concerned). A system of charging premiums was devised, so that insurers could accumulate funds to pay for eventual losses. As insurers grew, they accepted increasing numbers of risks, so that losses were bound to occur from time to time. It stands to reason that if you insure 100,000 houses, some of them are bound to suffer losses. Insurers were able to use statistical information, gathered from their experience of insuring many thousands of risks. This enabled them to refine their rating structures, to reflect more accurately the degree of hazard.

Returning to the parable, Fred thought it would be a good idea to formalise the insuring of the houses in the village. Farmer Giles had not been as generous as the other neighbours, and Fred began to wonder whether good neighbourliness would always come to the rescue in a crisis.

Fred formed a "club" into which every householder in the village paid weekly contributions. The money was put into the bank, where it earned interest, and gradually a fund was built up which would be enough to pay for

2 What is Reinsurance, and Why Do We Need It?

a new cottage and some furniture, should another fire occur. Even Farmer Giles became a member, because he feared that if he ever suffered a fire, his neighbours might recall how mean he had been to Fred, and refuse to help him.

When the people in the next village came to hear about Fred's scheme, they were eager to join, and soon Fred had a booming business. From time to time there were minor losses, but there was always enough money in the bank to meet the cost of repairs.

The story might have ended there, but for two things:

1. There was a severe windstorm, which resulted in so many lost roofs that Fred's company almost went out of business.
2. The company was asked to insure the Manor House, for a value many times greater than any of the cottages which were on the company's books at that time.

This is the nub of what reinsurance is all about. An insurer may well be capable of meeting all of its obligations arising out of everyday situations, but there are times when the insurer may be required to take on risks which are larger than usual, as well as there being the risk of the occasional event which gives rise to an unusual number of losses.

Let us look at these in greater detail:

1. Large risks

If a company insures several thousand buildings with values of around £100,000 and only one or two with values of £5 million the company's book of business (its "portfolio") is thrown out of balance by the larger risks.

The premium which the company receives for each of the smaller risks may be as little as £100. If one of the £5 million risks is totally destroyed, the company will lose the equivalent of the premiums from 50,000 smaller risks to pay for this single loss.

The company would be wise to purchase reinsurance on these larger risks, in order to protect itself against this kind of imbalance.

2. Catastrophic losses

In reinsurance terms, a catastrophe is a single event which results in losses affecting more than one insured risk.

Technically, a fire in one building which spreads to another building (where both are insured by the same company) is a catastrophe (in this case, a "conflagration").

More common examples of catastrophes are hurricanes, earthquakes, floods, winter freezing leading to burst pipes and water damage, etc.

In these kinds of event, each individual loss may be small (roof damage during a storm, for example) but the accumulated losses to the company may be many times the annual premiums collected.

These are the two most common factors which will prompt a company to purchase reinsurance. The company looks at the factors which expose it to higher degrees of hazard than it is capable of bearing. It then "lays off" this extra risk to other companies or underwriters, known as "reinsurers".

From here we can see the company's purpose in buying reinsurance: to stabilise its results over the long term in order to maintain profitability, by "ironing out" fluctuations in the underwriting result, caused by infrequent large losses. That is not to say that reinsurance exists to guarantee that the company will make a profit. Generally, however, if the company's business is profitable for 99 years out of 100, the company wants to put aside a little of that profit, in order to provide a buffer against the consequences of the odd bad year.

The purpose of buying reinsurance may be summarised as "stabilising results in order to protect the insurer's balance sheet". Reinsurance is not the only means of doing this; companies use various financial instruments, such as derivatives, currency dealings, interest rate swaps etc. Nevertheless, reinsurance (or "risk transfer") remains the most widely used means of protection against large swings in insurers' underwriting results.

So far, property insurance has been used in all of my examples. This is purely for simplicity's sake. Insurance is a diverse field, and it is amazing how many different types of risk are insurable. We shall deal with many of these later on in this book.

CHAPTER 2

TYPES OF REINSURANCE

Before dealing with the different types of reinsurance, let us look at another way of spreading a large risk. This method is older than reinsurance, and is known as "coinsurance". By this method, several insurance companies take shares of a risk, and the name of each insurer, as well as its share of the risk, will appear on the insurance policy.

This is commonly arranged by insurance brokers who fill a "slip" containing details of the risk. The broker takes the slip to a number of underwriters, who mark their acceptances on the slip. Each of these underwriters will enter into a contractual relationship with the insured party. A company which accepts a 10 per cent coinsurance share of a risk will only ever be liable for 10 per cent of any losses, even if some of the other coinsurers fail to pay their share.

Some insurance companies arrange coinsurance themselves, either on individual risks, or using prearranged business pooling arrangements with other companies.

Reinsurance differs from coinsurance in a number of ways, but perhaps the most important is that there is no contractual relationship between the direct insured and the reinsurer. There are separate contracts involved; one between the insured and the insurer, and another between the insurer and the reinsurer (see Figure 1).

From this figure, it can be seen that the insurer must pay all valid claims to the insured, irrespective of whether the insurer can recover from his reinsurers.

There are many types of reinsurance, but these can be broken down into two main groups; facultative and treaty. Within these groups there are various sub-divisions.

FACULTATIVE

Facultative is a term meaning "optional", and is usually used to describe the reinsurance of a single risk. It is optional upon both the insurer and the reinsurers: the insurer is at liberty to decide whether to buy reinsurance, how much and from whom; the reinsurers are at liberty to accept the risk or not.

In its simplest form, facultative reinsurance is very similar to coinsurance, except for the differences in contractual relationships mentioned above, as well

6 Types of Reinsurance

Figure 1: Coinsurance versus reinsurance

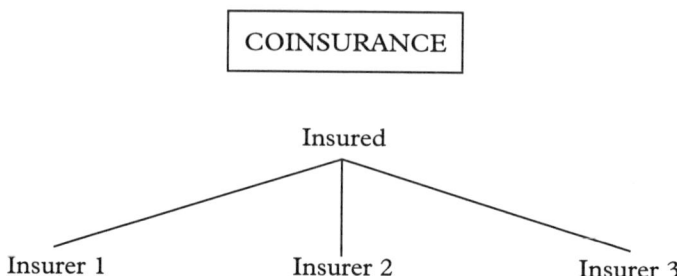

Contractual relationships are between the insured and each insurer separately. If one insurer fails to pay its share of a claim, the others are not liable for more than their own shares.

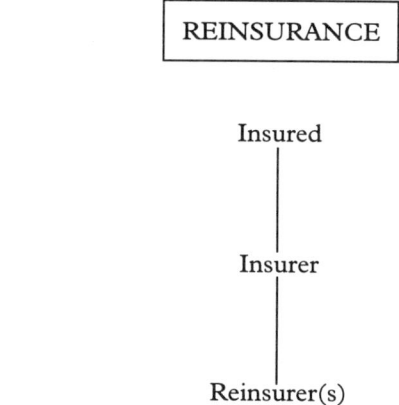

The insured only has a contractual relationship with the insurer. The insured is not a party to the contract between the insurer and the reinsurers. The insurer must pay valid claims, even if he fails to recover from his reinsurers.

as the payment of commission by the reinsurers to the insurer (in a reinsurance relationship, the insurer is known as the "Reinsured" or "Ceding Company").

This "ceding commission" is designed to reimburse the Ceding Company for the reinsurer's share of his acquisition costs (brokerage or agency commission paid by the Ceding Company to attract the business), as well as making a contribution towards the Ceding Company's other costs, such as administration, advertising etc.

If the insurer has paid away 20 per cent of the original gross premium as acquisition costs, and receives a total of 25 per cent ceding commission on the facultative reinsurance placement, the additional 5 per cent is referred to as "overriding commission", which is the contribution towards the Ceding Company's other costs referred to above. In theory, an insurer should not make a profit from reinsurance commission, but in reality, commission rates are used by reinsurers in a competitive way, and can often be highly advantageous to direct insurers as a way of improving net underwriting profit.

Facultative reinsurance may be split into two main categories: pro-rata (or proportional); and excess of loss (non-proportional).

Pro-rata (or proportional)

If the insurer covers a risk valued at £10 million but can only afford to lose £1 million in a single loss, it could buy reinsurance for 90 per cent of the risk.

The reinsurers would receive 90 per cent of the original gross premium (less their share of any premium tax as well as ceding commission at an agreed rate) and would reimburse the company for 90 per cent of all claims payments which the ceding company makes to the insured.

Just as in insurance, reinsurance is usually placed by way of a "slip" which is shown to prospective reinsurers, who will indicate whether they want to support the risk by "writing a line" on the slip. This is either carried around the market by a broker, sent to reinsurers' offices by facsimile or letter or, more recently, sent electronically to the market via a dedicated computer network.

In some cases, the facultative placement is followed up by a formal reinsurance policy document, known as a "full reinsurance policy", but these days most proportional facultative placements are formalised by a "slip policy", which is a pre-printed sticker attached to the slip, which states that the reinsurance follows the terms and conditions of the original policy, except where specifically amended by the slip conditions. This is a great time saver for brokers, because it means that the slip they prepare at the beginning of the placement becomes, in effect, the policy document.

The following is a typical slip for a pro-rata facultative reinsurance:

Broker's reference:	F13245
Type:	Fire, lightning and explosion reinsurance, as original
Form:	Slip Policy
Insured:	ABC Textiles, Limited
Reinsured:	XYZ Insurance Company Limited
Period:	12 months at 1 January 1996
Interest:	Building, Machinery and Contents of the Insured's textile mill

8 Types of Reinsurance

Sum Reinsured: 90% of £10,000,000 divided as follows:
Buildings: £3,000,000
Machinery: £4,000,000
Stocks: £6,000,000

Situation: Warrington Road, Derby, England

Conditions: Full Reinsurance Clause:
Being a reinsurance of, and warranted same gross rate, terms and conditions as and to follow the settlements of the Reinsured, and that said Reinsured retains during the currency hereof not less than 10% on identical subject matter and risk and in identically the same proportion of each separate part thereof, and in the event that the retained amount is less than stated above, reinsurers' lines hereon to be proportionately reduced.

Premium: Original Gross Rate: 2.25‰ (per mille)

Commission: 25% plus taxes as original

Brokerage: 5% of Gross Premium hereon

Information: Factory in operation since 1967
No known or reported losses to date.

The above slip is deliberately simple but, believe it or not, slips like this were placed in the market, not too many years ago. These days, reinsurers require far more information to enable them to evaluate a risk, and would want to see the latest survey report, so that they could get to know about the type of construction of the buildings, fire protection, housekeeping standards, machinery details etc.

The Full Reinsurance Clause looks a little Shakespearean these days, but is still in use in the London Market. Its purpose is to tie in the reinsurance contract to following the fortunes of the Ceding Company (Reinsured). In other words, the reinsurer is accepting responsibility for 90 per cent of the Reinsured's losses which affect the original policy, in return for which he will receive 90 per cent of the original gross premium. The 90 per cent share of the reinsurer covers all interests under the original policy; the Reinsured cannot choose to keep 100 per cent of the buildings item and nothing on the contents. This is what is meant by the words "and in identically the same proportion of each separate part thereof". The clause goes on to state the Reinsured's retention; this is used by reinsurers to gain an idea of what the Reinsured actually thinks of the risk. It is therefore made a condition of reinsurance that if, for example, the Reinsured states that he is retaining 10 per cent of the risk, and after a loss it transpires that he had placed another 5 per cent share elsewhere, resulting in a retention of only 5 per cent, the reinsurers would be entitled to pay only 50 per cent of their share of the loss. Without such a provision, it could be argued that the reinsurers could avoid any reinsurance on the grounds of misrepresentation, if it turned out that the Reinsured had retained less than the amount specified at the time of placement.

One thing which the Full Reinsurance Clause does not specify is what, if anything, reinsurers will contribute towards the Reinsured's expenses incurred in the settlement of claims (adjusters' fees etc.). Normal practice is that the reinsurers will pay their share of any costs incurred in the settlement of claims under the policy, provided that these have arisen solely as a result of the claim, and are not part of the Reinsured's day-to-day office expenses (such as the salaries of permanent employees). However, some larger companies now employ full time loss adjusters and legal advisers. These are "costed out" within the company, so that each division within the company pays for the service it receives. Such companies argue that these specialists are cheaper than employing outside companies to adjust and settle their claims. They therefore argue that such internal "billings" are a legitimate claims settlement expense, and that the reinsurers should pay their proportion. This argument is generally accepted by the reinsurance market.

Excess of loss (non-proportional)

Using the same example as the one above, the company might choose to pay the first £1 million of each loss affecting that risk, so that if there were a loss for £1.5 million the reinsurers would not pay 90 per cent of it, but only the amount which exceeds £1 million; in this case £500,000 or 33.33 per cent of the original loss. Most losses which affect property (and many other types of risk) are only partial, and it therefore follows that in paying the first £1 million of each loss, the insurer is likely to pay far more than 10 per cent of all losses affecting that risk. In fact, over the years the insurance industry has built up statistical tables to show what percentage of all loss payments relate to individual losses at varying percentages of the original insured values. Reinsurers do not charge pro-rata of the original premium for providing excess of loss coverage, because they are far less exposed to partial losses than the original insurer, who is picking up the bill for the more frequent small losses. Instead, the reinsurers charge a percentage of the original premium, calculated by reference to a table of "First Loss Discounts".

First Loss policies exist in direct insurance, where the Insured is reasonably certain that he could never suffer a loss for the full value of his insured property. Normally, if property is insured for less than its full value, a condition, known as "average" would apply in the event of a loss. For example, if the property value is £10 million but it is only insured for £5 million the insurers would apply average in the event of a partial claim, and would only pay 50 per cent of each claim. Their reasoning behind this is that, as the Insured only purchased insurance for 50 per cent of the true value (thereby only paying 50 per cent of the full premium), he had effectively chosen to insure himself for 50 per cent of the risk.

On the other hand, if the same Insured were to declare the correct value to the insurers, but take out a policy for only half the full value, the insurers could charge the premium based upon the full value, and then give the Insured a discount for the "top" 50 per cent of the risk, which the Insured is keeping for himself. This is called a First Loss Insurance, because the insurers will pay the first £5 million of each loss, and will not apply the condition of average.

Table 1 shows a typical First Loss Scale, although for simplicity's sake, the figures go up in stages of 10 per cent of insured value. In practice, the figures go up in 1 per cent increments, or smaller:

Table 1: A typical First Loss Scale

Percentage "First Loss" to "Declared full sum insured"	Premium as % of Original Gross Rate
10%	54%
20%	66%
30%	75%
40%	80%
50%	83%
60%	85%
70%	87%
80%	91%
90%	95%

In our example, the Insured has only bought insurance for up to 50 per cent of the declared full value, and would therefore only pay 83 per cent of the premium he would have been charged for a full value insurance. In effect, insurers are saying that an excess of loss coverage for 50 per cent in excess of the first 50 per cent would be worth 17 per cent of the "full value" premium.

Similar scales are used in excess of loss reinsurance. If the Insured had taken out a full value policy for £10 million and the insurer had decided to pay all losses up to £1 million it could decide to buy excess of loss reinsurance for £9 million excess of £1 million representing 90 per cent excess of 10 per cent of the original insured values. In theory, the reinsurance premium would be around 46 per cent of the original premium, and the insurer would keep 54 per cent of the original premium for undertaking to pay the first £1 million of each loss sustained. The reinsurance premium should be applied to the original premium net of the acquisition costs incurred by the insurer in obtaining the business, because the scale applies to the "pure risk premium". It should be stressed, however, that different reinsurers are likely to use different scales and, of course, the element of competition may lead a reinsurer to discount his rate more heavily than the scale would suggest.

It is noticeable from the following specimen slip that there is no ceding commission. This is because the reinsurance premium no longer follows the original rating. In effect, the reinsurer builds the commission into the reinsurance premium. Another factor to bear in mind is that a First Loss Scale will only hold good if the original rating is adequate. If the reinsurer feels that the original rate is only 50 per cent of the correct rate for the risk, he is likely to double the original rate before applying his excess of loss rating factor to it to arrive at his quotation of the reinsurance premium.

The following is a typical slip for an excess of loss facultative reinsurance:

Broker's reference: F13246

Type: Fire, lightning and explosion reinsurance, as original

Form: Full Policy

Insured: ABC Textiles, Limited

Reinsured: XYZ Insurance Company Limited

Period: 12 months at 1 January 1996

Interest: Building, Machinery and Contents of the Insured's textile mill

Sum Reinsured: £9,000,000 Ultimate Net Loss, each and every loss Excess of
£1,000,000 Ultimate Net Loss, each and every loss

In respect of an original sum insured of £10,000,000 divided as follows:
Buildings: £3,000,000
Machinery: £4,000,000
Stocks: £6,000,000

Situation: Warrington Road, Derby, England

Conditions: Ultimate Net Clause:

Premium: £8,280 adjustable at 36.8% of Original Gross Premium

Brokerage: 10% of Gross Premium hereon

Information: Factory in operation since 1967
No known or reported losses to date
Original Gross Rate 2.25‰ (per mille).

It can be seen that the reinsurance rate relates back to the original gross premium. In order to arrive at 36.8 per cent we have taken the original acquisition costs as being 20 per cent of the original premium. Hence the pure risk premium is £22,500 (2.25 per mille × £10 million) less 20 per cent = £18,000. We have then applied the 46 per cent figure from the scale to arrive at £8,280 which represents 36.8 per cent of the original gross premium of £22,500. The reason that the reinsurance premium is adjustable, is that the original premium may be adjusted during the period of the policy, for example, if stock values are declared monthly. In practice, an underwriter might load the excess of loss premium, in order to allow for his own expenses, profit margin and the amount paid to the broker for introducing the business.

The most important factor in an excess of loss reinsurance is the Ultimate Net Loss clause, which governs how the reinsurance will operate. There are many variations of this clause, but the following is a typical example:

"Ultimate Net Loss Clause
The term 'Ultimate Net Loss' shall mean the sum actually paid by the Reinsured in respect of any loss occurrence including expenses of litigation, if any, and all other loss expenses of the Reinsured (excluding, however, office expenses and salaries of officials of the company) but salvages and recoveries, including recoveries from other reinsurances shall first be deducted from such loss to arrive at the amount of liability, if any attaching hereunder.

All salvages, recoveries or payments recovered or received subsequent to any loss settlement hereunder shall be applied as if recovered or received prior to the aforesaid settlement, and all necessary adjustments shall be made by the parties hereto.

Nothing in this clause shall be construed as meaning that a recovery cannot be made hereunder until the Reinsured's Ultimate Net Loss has been ascertained."

Recently, there has been a great deal of legal argument over the words "actually paid" appearing in this clause. Traditionally, the view was that the words should be taken quite literally, in that the Insurer has to pay the loss, and only then could he recover from his reinsurers. However, it has been argued that this could lead to a situation in which reinsurers, faced with a large loss, could simply refuse to pay, in the hope that the Insurer would go into liquidation as a result. The view seems to have been upheld that, in the case of the insolvency of the Insurer, the company's liquidator will have full rights to reinsurance recoveries, even if the claims are unlikely to be paid in full to the original insureds, by virtue of the liquidation.[1] Of course the claim must be valid under the original policy, as well as under any separate conditions applicable to the reinsurance contract.

The other aspects of this clause deal with the establishment of what, precisely, constitutes the Ultimate Net Loss to the Reinsured. If, for example, the Reinsured had pro-rata reinsurance for 50 per cent of the risk, the recoveries under that reinsurance would be deducted from the Ultimate Net Loss, even if some of the reinsurers could not, or would not pay their share for whatever reason. Legal fees, adjusters' fees etc., could be treated as part of the original claim, but not the office expenses of the Reinsured or the salaries of the Reinsured's staff (however, please refer to the comment under pro-rata reinsurance about companies who use the services of "in-house" adjusters and legal departments).

---

1. *Charter Reinsurance Co. Ltd* v. *Lloyd's Syndicate 540 and 542—Patrick Feltrim Fagan.*

TREATIES

Facultative reinsurance is expensive to administer, because each risk must be individually negotiated. Similarly, each claim must be individually collected from the reinsurers.

Leaving aside historical accuracy, let us say that somebody had the bright idea of combining a number of different risks of similar characteristics, placing them all with one reinsurance market and generally streamlining the accounting and claims processes.

A facultative "lineslip" is one way of doing this, and many are still placed today. This is an agreement between a Ceding Company (direct insurer) and one or more reinsurers. Usually, the leading reinsurer will agree to all declarations to the cover on behalf of his fellow reinsurers. These kinds of agreement take many forms; some may stipulate that every reinsurer must agree all risks which are declared to the cover; others may provide for renewals of existing risks to be agreed automatically, provided there have been no major changes and no major losses. Reinsurance agreements are like fingerprints, in that no two are identical.

Other kinds of facultative facility include the "broker binder", where the broker may bind risks on behalf of underwriters, provided they fulfil certain criteria. Broker binders are quite often used in direct insurance, particularly motor business in the United Kingdom, but there are examples of broker binders in the field of reinsurance.

Unlike facultative facilities, treaties are strict agreements by the reinsurers to accept any risk underwritten by the Ceding Company, provided it falls within the treaty terms.

In almost every case, the Ceding Company is also obliged to cede every risk coming within the scope of the treaty.

(It should be noted here that the *ceding* of risks only happens in the case of pro-rata business. Excess of loss treaties *protect* the Reinsured against the occurrence of an event of a certain magnitude, and will be discussed later in this chapter. The term "Reinsured" refers to the direct insurer who is protected by reinsurance, and is a more appropriate term than "Ceding Company" when talking about excess of loss reinsurance. However, the terms "Reinsured", "Ceding Company", "Reassured" and "Client" are all used interchangeably in the reinsurance world.)

Treaties, therefore, are reinsurance agreements which are, for the most part, binding upon both the Reinsured and the reinsurers, to protect a certain type of insurance business, underwritten by the Reinsured. Like facultative reinsurances, they fall into the categories of pro-rata and excess of loss, but because we are dealing with large numbers of risks of different sizes and characteristics, these broad categories are further sub-divided.

14 Types of Reinsurance

Pro-rata Treaties

Sometimes referred to as "proportional treaties", these fall into three main types: Quota Share, Surplus and Facultative Obligatory.

Quota Share Treaties

These are agreements whereby the Reinsured is obliged to cede, and the reinsurer is obliged to accept a fixed percentage of all risks falling with the treaty terms. In the vast majority of cases, there is a maximum limit on the amount which may be ceded.

For example, if the reinsurers are committed to accept 90 per cent of up to £1 million per risk, everything is very simple for all risks whose insured value does not exceed that figure; but if the Reinsured has a risk where the sum insured is £2 million he must reinsure 50 per cent of it elsewhere, so that the Quota Share reinsurers will only receive 90 per cent of £1 million representing 45 per cent of the original sum insured.

The following is a simplified slip for a Property Quota Share Treaty:

Reinsured:	XXX Insurance Company, Barbados
Period:	Continuous contract, subject to 3 months notice of cancellation on 31 December of any year. Terms hereon from 1 January 1996.
Type:	Quota Share Treaty
Class:	All Fire and Allied Perils business written by the Reinsured in its Fire Department, including Burglary when written in conjunction with Fire, whether direct or by way of facultative reinsurance.
Territorial Scope:	Barbados and Barbadian interests abroad, where incidental
Limit:	To take up to 70% Quota Share of up to BD$10,000,000 Sum Insured any one risk. Reinsured retains 30% subject to excess of loss protection, if required.
Rate:	Original Gross Rates.
Commission:	37.5% but 30% for Earthquake.
Brokerage:	2.5% on Gross Ceded Premiums
Profit Commission:	25% (5% Reinsurers' expenses. Deficits carried forward a maximum of 3 years). Profit Commission calculation shall exclude Earthquake business.
Premium Reserve:	Nil

Loss Reserve:	Nil
Portfolio:	Premiums: 40% Outstanding Losses: 100% Annual clean cut basis, at the Reinsured's option.
Cash Loss:	BD$2,000,000 for ceded share.
Accounts:	Quarterly.
General Conditions:	Excluding treaty and excess of loss reinsurance. Nuclear Energy Risks Exclusion Clause (Reinsurance) NMA 1975(a). Aggregate cession limit BD$10,000,000,000 for 70% ceded share.
Wording:	As expiring. Any amendments to be agreed, Leading Underwriter only.
Information:	Information package dated 15th November, 1995 seen by Reinsurers. Estimated Premium Income 1996: BD$40,500,000 for ceded share.

Note that we are at pains to specify that amounts in the treaty are for the 70 per cent ceded share, rather than 100 per cent. A confusing situation can arise with Quota Share Treaties if all interested parties are not absolutely clear about what amount they are protecting. Sometimes a broker might receive an order to place 70 per cent of the treaty. He has the option of placing lines totalling 70 per cent of the 100 per cent limit, or lines totalling 100 per cent of the 70 per cent limit. If the broker places lines totalling 70 per cent the client might take this as being 70 per cent of the 70 per cent Quota Share. He might then award the other 30 per cent to another broker or place it directly himself. The broker may be under the impression that his 70 per cent order is based on the 100 per cent limit, and the contract will then be over-placed. The opposite may also occur, leaving the Reinsured with insufficient cover.

Surplus Treaties

A Surplus Treaty is an agreement which covers all insured risks which have sums insured above a specified amount. The maximum amount which may be ceded to a Surplus Treaty in respect of any single risk is governed by the retention of the Ceding Company. The retention (the amount kept by the Ceding Company), is also known as the company's "line", which may be either gross or net.

Where the company uses a Quota Share Treaty, a "Gross Line" is the 100 per cent amount ceded to the Quota Share Treaty (including the Ceding Company's retention proper). Hence, if the company has an underlying Quota Share Treaty with a 100 per cent limit of £1 million and a Surplus Treaty with a limit of 10 Gross Lines, the effective limit of the Surplus Treaty is £10 million. However, in order for the Surplus Treaty to take the full £10 million there would need to be a full cession of £1 million to the Quota Share Treaty. Naturally, the original sum insured would also need to be £11 million or more. If, because of some condition in the Quota Share Treaty, it could only take £500,000 for 100 per cent, the Surplus Treaty could only take up to £5 million. Similarly, if the Sum Insured were £6 million and the Quota Share Treaty took £1 million the Surplus Treaty could only take five Gross Lines, because that is all that would be left.

In the vast majority of cases, the retention of the Ceding Company is governed by a table of limits, which grades risk according to their perceived degree of hazard. For example, a residential risk, such as an apartment block of first class construction may be regarded as the best type of risk from the point of view of fire hazard. The retention on such a risk would therefore be 100 per cent of the agreed maximum. On the other hand, a sawmill, constructed of timber, might be considered such a poor risk that the allowable retention according to the table of retentions might only be 10 per cent of the agreed maximum.

Going back to the £1 million Quota Share Treaty, the maximum amount which the company is allowed to cede in respect of such a sawmill would be only £100,000 and, consequently, the maximum cession to a 10 Gross Line Surplus Treaty would be £1 million.

Often, companies do not have a Quota Share Treaty at all. In such cases, the limits of their Surplus Treaties would be expressed as numbers of "Net Lines", one "Net Line" being the amount retained by the Ceding Company on a particular risk.

The following slip would be typical:

Reinsured: XXX Insurance Company, Barbados

Period: Continuous contract, subject to 3 months notice of cancellation to 31 December of any year.
Terms hereon from 1 January 1996.

Type: First Surplus Treaty

Class: All Fire and Allied Perils business written by the Reinsured in its Fire Department, including Burglary when written in conjunction with Fire, whether direct or by way of facultative reinsurance.

Territorial Scope: Barbados and Barbadian interests abroad, where incidental.

Limit: To take up to 10 Gross Lines of up to BD$10,000,000 per line, Sum Insured any one risk.
Maximum cession hereto BD$100,000,000 Sum Insured any one risk, surplus to the Reinsured's Quota Share Treaty.

Rate:	Original Gross Rates.
Commission:	35% but 30% for Earthquake.
Brokerage:	2.5% on Gross Ceded Premiums
Profit Commission:	25% (5% Reinsurers' expenses. Deficits carried forward a maximum of 3 years). Profit Commission calculation shall exclude Earthquake business.
Premium Reserve:	Nil
Loss Reserve:	Nil
Portfolio	Premiums: 40% Outstanding Losses: 100% Annual clean cut basis, at the Reinsured's option.
Cash Loss:	BD$2,000,000 for Treaty share.
Accounts:	Quarterly.
General Conditions:	Excluding treaty and excess of loss reinsurance. Nuclear Energy Risks Exclusion Clause (Reinsurance) NMA 1975(a). Aggregate cession limit BD$40,000,000,000
Wording:	As expiring. Any amendments to be agreed, Leading Underwriter only.
Information:	Information package dated 15 November 1995 seen by Reinsurers. Estimated Premium Income 1996: BD$100,000,000

It would be usual to combine the Quota Share and Surplus Treaties into one slip, or at least place the two in conjunction. In such circumstances the Profit Commission would normally be based upon the combined results of the Quota Share and Surplus(es).

Facultative Obligatory covers

A Facultative Obligatory cover may seem like a contradiction in terms. The word "Facultative", as we have already seen, implies an option. This means, in this context, that the Ceding Company has the option of whether to cede risks to the cover or otherwise. "Obligatory" refers to the obligation of the reinsurers to accept whatever risks are ceded, provided they fit in with the terms and conditions of the cover itself.

Cessions to a Facultative Obligatory cover need not bear any relationship to the level of the Ceding Company's retention. Hence, in the case of a sawmill, where the Quota Share cession is £100,000 a 10 line Surplus Treaty could

18 Types of Reinsurance

only accept £1 million even if the treaty limit for top quality risks were £10 million. On the other hand, a Facultative Obligatory cover with a limit of £10 million could accept that amount on a sawmill, just as easily as on an apartment block. This sums up the difficulties of placing Facultative Obligatory covers. A Facultative Obligatory cover is usually capable of taking much more of the hazardous risks than the Surplus Treaty, but it will receive less of the better quality risks, which are usually gobbled up by the underlying Quota Share and Surplus Treaties. This usually results in such covers having a low premium income in relation to the maximum cession limit, so that when a large loss does occur, it takes away the profits of many good years.

Here is a typical slip:

Reinsured: XXX Insurance Company, Barbados

Period: Continuous contract, subject to 3 months notice of cancellation to 31 December of any year
Terms hereon from 1 January 1996.

Type: Facultative Obligatory Treaty

Class: All Fire and Allied Perils business written by the Reinsured in its Fire Department, including Burglary when written in conjunction with Fire, whether direct or by way of facultative reinsurance

Territorial Scope: Barbados and Barbadian interests abroad, where incidental

Limit: To take up to BD$100,000,000 Sum Insured any one risk

Rate: Original Gross Rates

Commission: 30%

Brokerage: 2.5% on Gross Ceded Premiums

Profit Commission: Nil

Premium Reserve: Nil

Loss Reserve: Nil

Portfolio: Premiums: 40%
Outstanding Losses: 100%
Annual clean cut basis, at the Reinsured's option

Cash Loss: BD$2,000,000 for Treaty share

Accounts: Quarterly

General Conditions:	Excluding treaty and excess of loss reinsurance. Nuclear Energy Risks Exclusion Clause (Reinsurance) NMA 1975(a). Aggregate cession limit BD$3,000,000,000
Wording:	As expiring. Any amendments to be agreed, Leading Underwriter only.
Information:	Information package dated 15 November 1995 seen by Reinsurers. Estimated Premium Income 1996: BD$25,000,000 for ceded share.

Cessions to treaties

Cessions to pro-rata treaties begin with the establishment by the Ceding Company of its retention for the risk in question. As already mentioned, this retention or "line" may either be gross (involving a Quota Share Treaty) or net. The retention for the risk is usually governed by a table of retentions (sometimes known as a "line guide") which classifies risks according to the degree of hazard. For fire and allied perils business, this can mean occupancy (the Insured's activities), construction and location (where there are differing levels of catastrophe hazard).

Having established the retention, the treaties are "filled" in sequence (see Figure 2), until the sum insured has been fully allocated over the treaty programme. If the capacity of the treaty programme is less than the sum insured, the Company may then seek facultative reinsurance for the balance.

Once the cessions to each treaty are established, they are converted into percentages of the risk in question, and each treaty will then receive that percentage of the premiums and will pay the same percentage of any claims which may occur under the policy.

Special considerations

It should be noted that the structure shown above is quite simple, although typical of many small companies' treaty programmes. However, there is great variety in the structure and operation of reinsurance programmes, and some of the more common variations are described below.

Basis of cession

So far we have talked about ceding risks based upon the original sum insured. There are several other ways of making cessions to treaties, such as the following.

20 Types of Reinsurance

Figure 2: The sequence for filling treaties

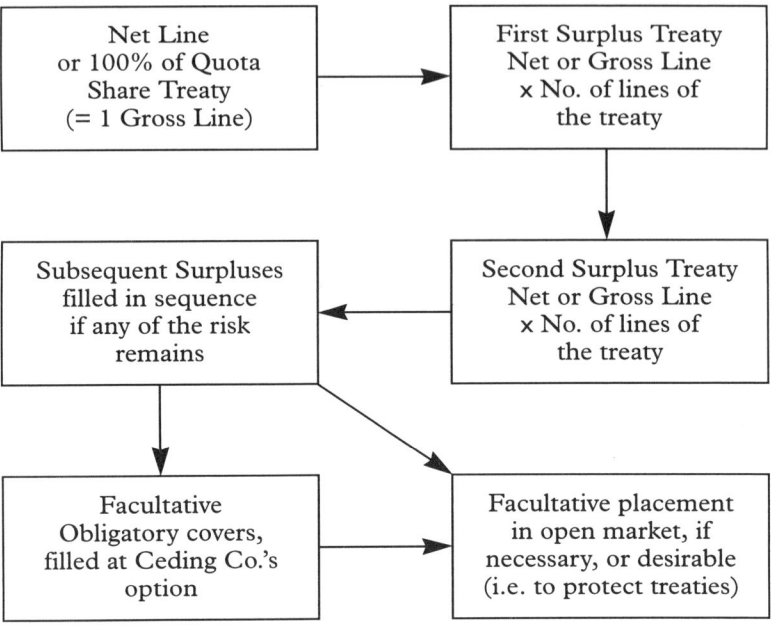

Top Location and pro-rata basis

This is, in practice, how a Sum Insured Treaty operates. Many insured risks are not confined to a single location. A modern industrial risk may be made up of multiple locations. The value of the highest valued location ("Top Location") may be only £10 million but the value of the entire "schedule" may be many times that figure. In such circumstances, a treaty with a capacity of £10 million Sum Insured, any one risk, could absorb the entire policy. The cession would be made based upon the sum insured at the top location, and the same percentage would be ceded of all the lesser locations. This is preferable to trying to cede each individual location separately, because certain items may be difficult to allocate between separate locations (e.g. floating stock items, moveable plant, profits etc.).

PML basis

PML stands for "Probable Maximum Loss". This is an assessment made by a surveyor as to the worst loss which in his opinion, the risk would sustain, and usually assumes that at least some of the risk prevention measures, such as fire walls and sprinkler systems are operational. If a treaty programme is designed to accept risks on a PML basis, and has a limit of £10 million PML, then a risk with a sum insured of £20 million may be fully ceded to the treaty, provided its PML does not exceed 50 per cent of the total sum insured.

Treaties which accept cessions on a PML basis usually contain a condition that the PML used in calculating the treaty cession will not fall below a certain figure. Minimum PML figures are typically in the region of 25–50 per cent so that, in the case of a 25 per cent minimum PML, the treaty could only accept up to four times its PML limit, based on the sum insured of any one risk. This would prevent a cession of £1,000 million being made to a treaty with a £10 million limit, if a risk should only carry a 1 per cent PML. PML figures have been known to be seriously underestimated, as was the case with the famous explosion loss at Flixborough in the early 1970s. A figure of around 15 per cent had been proposed, but the plant was totally destroyed in the explosion, which also caused significant damage to neighbouring property.

If the treaty is on a PML basis, and the policy covers multiple locations, the principle of "Top and Pro-rata" is applied to the PMLs of each location. Here, the cession to treaties would be based on the highest PML, which is not necessarily the location with the highest insured values.

Per policy basis

This is often seen on Marine Cargo treaties and is in response to the fact that many different cargoes, belonging to a variety of Insureds, covered by several insurers, and bound for different ports, may all end up on the same vessel at a given time. Some insurers find it impossible to know, with any certainty, how much exposure they have on a particular vessel. This kind of treaty gives the insurer the comfort of unlimited protection for its commitments on any vessel, although the insurer still has to be careful about the accumulation of his retentions. This is usually taken care of by excess of loss protections.

Per bottom basis

This again refers to Marine Cargo treaties. A "bottom" is any kind of vessel or other carrying conveyance. On such treaties, the Ceding Company is obliged to maintain records of his commitments on each vessel. This is often difficult to achieve, because in many cases, not even the consignee knows which vessel his cargo is on until after it has arrived. Trans-shipment is a common maritime practice, in which a cargo is transferred from its original carrying vessel to another vessel in mid-voyage. This can make the job of monitoring per-vessel accumulations even more difficult.

Per vessel basis

This is used for Marine Hull treaties. Cessions are made based upon the insured value of the hull and machinery. It should be noted that a Marine Hull policy does not only cover the hull and machinery, but also certain liabilities, such as liability for the running down of other vessels; ships' crews' personal effects, employers' liability etc. This can give rise to a single loss of more than the treaty limit, if a claim involves more than one section of an original policy.

Where a fleet of vessels is covered by one policy, it is often the practice to cede each vessel separately, to make full use of the treaty capacity. This is an aspect of Marine market practice which differs considerably from its Non-Marine counterpart. If the treaty limit applies per vessel, the reinsurers will expect a full cession of each vessel under a policy, as opposed to non-marine practice, which would allow the cession to be made based upon the value of the largest individual risk in the policy schedule, with pro-rata of lesser valued risks.

Per person basis

Personal Accident treaties (or treaties with a Personal Accident section) are usually limited to a maximum sum insured per person. This is based upon the "capital sum" for the person concerned (i.e. the sum payable in the event of the Insured's death). There is usually a further limit within the treaty for "known accumulations" (e.g. five times the "per person" limit). This is designed to limit the reinsurers' maximum exposure on a single aeroplane, ship or vehicle. Normally, groups of people in a single building are not regarded as known accumulations for reinsurance purposes. Also, known accumulations relate to Group Personal Accident policies covering one insured organisation. In such cases, it is usual for the original policy to contain an accumulation limit, per aircraft or other conveyance. It would obviously be impossible for an insurer to know about a situation in which two of its policyholders had several employees on the same aeroplane, or if a number of individual insureds were travelling together. These are examples of unknown accumulations, which could give rise to catastrophic losses to both the insurer and its reinsurers alike. This is precisely why reinsurance is so necessary for a Personal Accident portfolio.

Having established the percentage of a risk to be ceded to the various proportional treaties, these cession percentages are then maintained throughout the policy period. However, the sum insured may be increased during the period of the policy, and this could result in the treaty limits being exceeded for that risk. There are several ways to deal with such a situation:

1. The Ceding Company could recalculate the cession percentages from the effective date of the increase. Any losses occurring on or after that date would be allocated using the new percentages.
2. The treaty may contain a condition allowing for such increases in original policy limits, after they have been ceded. Typically, a maximum increase of 10 per cent above treaty limits would be allowable.

3. The Ceding Company may build a safety margin into its cession strategy, so that only 90 per cent of the treaty limits are utilised at the beginning of each policy period.

PRACTICAL EXERCISE 1: DISTRIBUTION OF PREMIUMS AND CLAIMS OVER A PROPORTIONAL PROGRAMME

When ceding a risk to treaties, the first thing to do is to establish the company's retention. Normally, this is done by referring to a table of retentions, which grades risk according to occupancy, construction and catastrophe zone.

Table 2: Specimen Table of Retentions (simplified)

Construction/Occupancy	1	2	3	4
A	100%	80%	70%	60%
B	80%	70%	60%	50%
C	70%	60%	50%	40%
D	60%	50%	40%	30%

Occupancy: refers to the type of risk. For example, apartments or condominiums might appear under Occupancy Class A, whereas a Class D occupancy might include an oil refinery.

Construction: means how the insured buildings are made. For example, Construction Class 1 would refer to buildings made of steel and concrete. A wooden building would be regarded as Construction Class 4. Therefore, on a category A risk, of Class 1 construction, the company would take a maximum retention, but on a category D risk, of Class 4 construction, the company would only retain 30 per cent of its normal maximum retention.

Retention: can be either gross or net. If the company uses a Quota Share Treaty, the retention may be expressed as a gross amount, meaning the 100 per cent amount ceded to the Quota Share Treaty. This is then known as a *Gross Line*. Cessions to the Surplus Treaties are then based on this Gross Line. For example, if the limit of the Quota Share Treaty is $1 million for 100 per cent and the First Surplus Treaty has a limit of 10 Gross Lines, the Surplus Treaty can accept up to $10 million for a Class A risk of 1st Class construction, but it would only be able to accept up to $3 million for a Class D risk of 4th Class construction.

Net Line: If there is no Quota Share Treaty, the company's retention is known as a Net Line. The Surplus Treaty limits are then expressed as numbers of Net Lines.

Facultative Obligatory Cover has a monetary limit per risk, independent of the company's retention. Therefore, if a company had a Facultative Obligatory cover, with a limit of $10 million, it could cede $10 million in respect of a Category D risk of 4th Class construction, as well as a Category A risk of 1st Class construction.

A company has the following programme:

Quota Share Treaty	(30% retained)	1,000,000
First Surplus	10 Gross Lines	10,000,000
Second Surplus	10 Gross Lines	10,000,000
Facultative Obligatory Cover		10,000,000

The company uses the specimen table of retentions given above.

Allocate the following risks over the above treaty programme and distribute the premiums and claims in the same proportion as the Sum Insured. (See Appendix 1 for answers to Practical Exercise 1.)

1. Occupancy Category: A
   Construction Class: 1
   Sum Insured: $25,000,000
   Premium: $50,000
   Claim: $35,000

2. Occupancy Category: C
   Construction Class: 3
   Sum Insured: $20,000,000
   Premium: $58,000
   Claim: $39,000

3. Occupancy Category: B
   Construction Class: 3
   Sum Insured: $15,000,000
   Premium: $38,000
   Claim: $350,000

4. Occupancy Category: A
   Construction Class: 3
   Sum Insured: $18,000,000
   Premium: $36,000
   Claim: $15,000

CHAPTER 3

TREATY REINSURANCE—FINANCIAL ASPECTS

As we have already seen, a reinsurance treaty is a financial arrangement between the Ceding Company and one or more reinsurers.

Such a treaty may also be regarded as a form of business partnership in which the Ceding Company uses its local knowledge and resources in order to underwrite a book of business which he shares with his reinsurers.

The Ceding Company may be underwriting many risks on a daily basis and frequently paying claims. It would be a very cumbersome exercise to distribute the moneys to the reinsurers on an individual transaction basis. A Ceding Company will therefore maintain records of the individual transactions, and periodically issue an account to its reinsurers (or reinsurance broker) summarising the transactions for a given period.

Usually treaty accounts are issued every three months, but some treaties may specify half-yearly or even annual accounts.

A treaty account statement will show the total amount of premium which has been collected on behalf of the reinsurers, as well as the reinsurers' share of all claims payments. However, premiums and claims are not the whole story, and a reinsurance treaty accounts statement will often contain many other accounting provisions which are directly related to the conditions stipulated at the time the treaty was placed.

Such provisions will include some or all of the following:

Credited to the reinsurers

1. Premiums, net of returns and cancellations.
2. Premium Reserve Released.
3. Loss Reserve Released.
4. Interest on Reserves.
5. Premium Portfolio Incoming.
6. Loss Portfolio Incoming.
7. Refund of Cash Losses.

Debited to the reinsurers

1. Ceding Commission.

2. Tax on Premiums.
3. Premium Reserve Retained.
4. Loss Reserve Retained.
5. Paid Claims.
6. Premium Portfolio Withdrawal.
7. Loss Portfolio Withdrawal.
8. Profit Commission.

Many of the items shown under the credit section, can sometimes appear as debits and vice versa. For example, the premiums ceded during the period of the account might be negative, if there have been large returns of premium, due to the cancellation of some policies, or other reasons. In this case, the premium will be debited to the reinsurers, whilst the corresponding items of commission, tax and premium reserve retained will be credits, rather than debits. Similarly, there may be large claims recoveries, due to *salvage* or *subrogation*, which may result in a net refund of claims to the reinsurers.

Let us look at some of these items in detail.

PREMIUMS

As we have already seen, whenever the Ceding Company underwrites an individual *risk*, it must establish how much of the risk it can bear for its *net account*. This *retention* is decided by reference to the company's *table of limits* which takes into account certain factors concerning the quality of the risk. Such factors may include the type of property covered, the use to which it is put, construction standards, risk protection measures, location, etc.

Having established the level of its retention, the Ceding Company then makes a cession to the treaties. The cessions to the various treaties (and facultative reinsurances, where applicable) are converted into percentages of the original policy limits. Each treaty is then credited with its percentage share of all premiums charged under that policy. These premium allocations are entered by the Ceding Company into a *register of cessions* and at the end of the specified accounting period, the premiums from this register are totalled, and credited to the reinsurers in the technical accounting statement.

All premium transactions are dealt with in this way. Very often, an insurance policy will be taken out for a period of one year, and a single premium will be charged at the beginning of the year. In other cases, however, premiums are slightly more complex. For example, a commercial or industrial concern may take out an insurance to cover all of its property against the risks of Fire and Allied Perils. This property may include stocks of raw materials and finished goods, whose amounts and values fluctuate seasonally. It is common practice to insure such items on a monthly declaration basis. The Insured may pay an initial premium based on an average anticipated stock value (i.e. the total of the estimated monthly stock values for the coming year, divided by 12).

Alternatively, the premium may be initially taken at 75 per cent of the highest anticipated value. The Insured will then submit declarations to the insurer, of the value of the stocks on a given day each month. At the end of the period, the insurer will calculate the average of the 12 monthly declarations, and apply the premium rate to the resultant figure. If the premium calculated in this way is higher than the *deposit premium* which was charged at the beginning of the year, the Insured will be charged an additional premium. If it is lower, some premium will be refunded. There are many other ways in which premium transactions may take place in respect of a policy, either during the policy period or shortly after it has expired, and the reinsurers will be debited or credited with their share of all of these in the corresponding technical account.

Commission

Ceding Commission is the amount the reinsurers pay to the Ceding Company for introducing the business. Often, it is calculated as a flat percentage of the premiums ceded to the reinsurers, net of returns and cancellations. Sometimes, however, it is calculated on a *sliding scale*, which is governed by the *loss ratio* of the treaty. The loss ratio is the percentage of the incurred losses over the gross ceded premiums.

A typical sliding scale commission may look like the following:

"40% commission at a loss ratio of 50% or less, reducing by 0.5% for every 1% increase in the Loss Ratio to 30% at a loss ratio of 70% or greater. Provisional commission 35%.

Definitions:

Loss Ratio
The percentage of incurred losses to Gross Earned Premium for the period under consideration.

Incurred Losses
The reinsurers' share of paid losses, debited to them during the period under consideration, less the incoming Loss Portfolio transfer, plus the outgoing Loss Portfolio Transfer.

Gross Earned Premium
The Reinsurers' share of the gross premiums ceded to them during the period under consideration, plus the incoming Premium Portfolio, less the outgoing Premium Portfolio."

Sometimes the definitions may vary. For example, the above calculation would apply to a treaty which is *Clean-cut*. Other treaties may operate on an *underwriting year basis*, where portfolio transfer provisions do not apply. In such cases, incurred losses may be defined as paid plus outstanding losses, while Earned Premiums will be the ceded premiums, less a provision for the unearned portion of the premiums at the end of the year.

Some sliding scale calculations will be adjusted annually, until all liabilities for the period in question have been discharged. Others may specify a once-

and-for-all calculation for each annual period of the treaty. Often, there is a provision that if the loss ratio for a particular year is unusually high, an agreed amount of losses will be carried forward to the calculations for subsequent years, until the loss ratio returns to a certain level. There are infinite variations.

Tax

Reinsurers are expected to pay their share of any taxes levied upon premiums which the Ceding Company receives. It should be noted, however, that the reinsurers are not responsible for any part of other taxes for which the Ceding Company may be liable, such as corporation tax on the company's profits. In some countries, the Fire Brigade is funded either by a levy on premiums, or by a kind of tax on premiums (*Fire Brigade Charges*). Fire Brigade Charges are recognised as a legitimate deduction, for which reinsurers may be debited with their share. On the other hand, the Ceding Company may simply charge a levy separately, and pay it directly to the local authority, without putting it through the reinsurers' books.

PREMIUM RESERVES

Premium reserves are a common feature of proportional treaties, although these days, their original function seems to be overlooked. Originally, premium reserves were put into treaties in order to protect the Ceding Company against the inability of the reinsurers to pay claims. The reasoning was that if the Ceding Company retains from the ceded reinsurance premiums, sufficient to cover the unexpired liability of policies in force, then in the event that the reinsurers become insolvent, or unable to pay claims for some other reason, the Ceding Company could purchase new reinsurance with the retained premium, or alternatively meet the reinsurers' share of future claims out of the premium reserve it was withholding.

In other words, premium reserves were designed as a form of security against the non-performance of reinsurers. Many reinsurers these days argue that this is no longer a justifiable reason for holding onto their money, because in many cases, the reinsurance company may have many times the assets of the Ceding Company, leading them to argue that their security is better than that of the Ceding Company. Even Lloyd's underwriters, who are not capitalised in the same way that companies are, could argue against having premium reserves withheld from them, because they are already contributing large amounts to various *Premium Trust Funds*, and are therefore, in effect, putting up reserves twice over.

Many national governments require that insurance companies operating within their jurisdiction maintain a certain level of premium reserve to cover their own unexpired liabilities. Some governments go further, and stipulate that all foreign reinsurers must allow their Ceding Companies to retain premium reserves at a specified level. In some countries, there is a two-tier system for premium reserves. Licensed or *admitted* reinsurers are recognised as properly funded, reserved and regulated. They are therefore not required to grant further reserves to Ceding Companies in that country. On the other hand, foreign reinsurers who are not licensed or admitted must deposit premium reserves with the Ceding Companies.

Clearly, it is advantageous to any Ceding Company to retain premium reserves, as they provide an additional source of funds which may be invested. In recent years, there has been a move against granting premium reserves, unless the reinsurers are required by law to grant them. On the other hand, it is recognised that this is an attractive provision from the point of view of the Ceding Company, and in a softening market, some reinsurers may start to grant reserves as a way of attracting or retaining business.

Sometimes, reinsurers may supply the Ceding Company with a *Letter of Credit* instead of providing reserves in cash. A letter of credit is a kind of promissory note issued by a bank, which guarantees that if the reinsurer should default, the bank will pay the Ceding Company up to the specified amount. The advantage of this to the reinsurer is that he pays a flat fee to the bank for the service, and retains the rest of the money himself. This is fine, provided that the Ceding Company plays fairly, and does not immediately "call" the Letter of Credit. If the LOC is "called" the issuing bank must immediately pay the called amount to the beneficiary (in this case the Ceding Company) and will debit the reinsurer's account immediately. This rarely happens in practice, but insurance policies are available to protect the reinsurers against the financial effects of "unfair calling".

LOSS RESERVES

Loss reserves have exactly the same purpose as premium reserves, in that they are intended to secure the Ceding Company against the possible non-performance of the reinsurers. Loss reserves cover those losses which have already occurred, but have not been paid by the Ceding Company as at a particular date (usually the anniversary date of the treaty).

Again, national governments often require any insurance company within its jurisdiction to constitute a reserve for losses which have occurred but which are, as yet, unpaid. Some governments place a requirement upon the insurance company to obtain from their reinsurers their share of such outstanding losses.

Loss reserves may sometimes be inflated by a factor called "IBNR", meaning *Incurred But Not Reported*. This refers to the fact that, at any given date, there may be losses for which the Ceding Company (and in turn, its reinsurers) may be liable, which have already occurred, but of which the Ceding Company presently has no knowledge. The amount of IBNR is likely to be relatively small for simple classes of business, such as Fire, because insurers will usually be aware of most losses within a few days of their occurrence. On the other hand, some liability policies may incur losses which only come to light several years after the occurrence. The methods of calculating IBNR are many and complicated. Often they are the result of the Ceding Company's experience of a particular class of business, based on observations of how the incurred loss position of their account develops over time.

The important thing is that the Ceding Company should be consistent in its approach to calculating IBNR, where it is including such a factor in its loss reserve which is withheld from the reinsurers. If the Ceding Company wishes to introduce any change in its method of calculation, it should discuss the matter with its reinsurers, and obtain their approval. Few reinsurers are prepared to allow IBNR unless it is a legal requirement.

Both premium and loss reserves are useful, not only for the Ceding Companies, who have the use of the money it is withholding, but are also viewed by some governments as useful ways of slowing down the movement of currency abroad.

INTEREST ON RESERVES

As the Ceding Company is holding onto its reinsurers' money in the form of premium and loss reserves, reinsurers often demand interest at a specified rate. This rate is often between 2.5 and 5 per cent and never seems to vary much or to bear any relation to the prevailing market interest rate. However, this is once again dictated by reinsurance market conditions, and rates may increase during a hardening market and reduce when there is more competition for proportional treaty business.

An often overlooked factor is the effect of currency devaluation on the value of reserves retained. A 12-month delay in receiving 40 per cent of one's premium could render it virtually valueless by the time it is received. It should also be noted that premium reserves are taken on Gross Premiums. In other words, if the treaty conditions stipulate 40 per cent Ceding Commission and 40 per cent premium reserve, the reinsurers will only receive 20 per cent of the ceded premiums during the first year.

Sometimes reinsurers stipulate that reserves must be constituted in hard currency, such as United States dollars, in order to protect them against the effects of devaluation of the Ceding Company's national currency.

HOW RESERVES ARE ACCOUNTED

Taking the example of a new treaty, with premium reserves taken at 40 per cent, loss reserves at 100 per cent of the outstanding losses at the anniversary date, and interest calculated at 4 per cent per annum, the treaty account might look like Table 3.

Table 3: A sample treaty account

Year 1

Period	Item	Debit	Credit
1st Quarter	Premium		100,000
	Premium Res. Retained	40,000	
2nd Quarter	Premium		120,000
	Premium Res. Retained	48,000	
3rd Quarter	Premium		90,000
	Premium Res. Retained	36,000	
4th Quarter	Premium		60,000
	Premium Res. Retained	24,000	
	Loss Res. Retained	23,000	

Year 2

Period	Item	Debit	Credit
5th Quarter	Premium		50,000
	Premium Res. Retained	20,000	
	Premium Res. Released		40,000
	Interest		1,600
6th Quarter	Premium		10,000
	Premium Res. Retained	4,000	
	Premium Res. Released		48,000
	Interest		1,920
7th Quarter	Premium Returned	1,000	
	Premium Res. Retained		400
	Premium Res. Released		36,000
	Interest		1,440
8th Quarter	Premium		200
	Premium Res. Retained	80	
	Premium Res. Released		24,000
	Loss Res. Released		23,000
	Interest		1,880
	Loss Res. Retained	12,000	

In the above example, we can see that the loss reserve at the end of the first year was 23,000 and that this amount was debited to reinsurers in the fourth quarterly account. It was refunded to reinsurers one year later, and reinsurers received the annual rate of interest on the money which had been withheld. However, at the end of the second year, there were still outstanding losses under the treaty, and so a new loss reserve figure was constituted.

We can also see that throughout the second year, the policies ceded to the treaty were still generating premium transactions, all of which need to be reflected in the reserve account. The reserving process needs to continue until the reserve account has a zero balance. Only the amounts of reserve retained and released form part of the reserve account. The premiums and Interest items would appear in the technical account only.

LOSSES

Whenever the Ceding Company pays a claim to one of its policyholders, it will calculate the share payable by its reinsurers based upon the same percentages it used when calculating reinsurers' share of the premium for that policy. These amounts will be entered into a register of paid losses and incorporated into the next technical account which is sent to the reinsurers. The Ceding Company will include any amounts which it has had to pay to loss adjusters, solicitors and other professionals in connection with the claim, so that the reinsurers will pay their share of such claims expenses. Similarly, if the Ceding Company subsequently recovers a part of the claim by virtue of salvage or subrogation, the reinsurers are entitled to their share of these recoveries. *Salvage* means the residual value of the damaged property. Once an insurer has paid a claim in respect of damaged property, the property is then owned by the insurer, who may dispose of it how he wishes. This is usually by way of a salvage sale, although sometimes the policyholder might take back the damaged goods and the original claim payment is adjusted accordingly.

Subrogation occurs when the insurer pays a claim to his policyholder, even though another person may be legally liable for the loss. After paying the claim, the insurer is entitled to take over the legal rights of the policyholder and may then sue the party who was responsible for the loss. Any amount recovered in this way, net of legal fees, should be shared with reinsurers in proportion to their liability.

Similar to subrogation is *contribution* which occurs when the policyholder has a number of policies which could pay his claim. Insurance policies normally contain a proviso that if there are other policies in force covering the same interest, all policies should contribute towards any loss. Naturally, reinsurers would expect to share the proceeds of any contributions from other policies which might result in a reduced claim to the policy they are reinsuring.

CASH LOSS REFUNDS

Imagine a treaty which commences on 1 January and has a provision for quarterly submission of technical accounts within 60 days of the close of the quarter, and settlement by the debtor party within a further 30 days.

Cash Loss Refunds

If the Ceding Company had to pay a claim on 2 January, it would not be able to collect the money from its reinsurers for almost another six months (90 days after the close of the first quarter).

If the amount involved is large, this could put a severe strain upon the company's cash flow. Given that the whole purpose of reinsurance is to protect the company's balance sheet, it is clearly not the reinsurers' intention to starve the company of cash flow when a large loss occurs. In order to prevent such a situation from arising, many treaties contain a provision known as "cash loss" whereby the reinsurers agree that claims payments above a certain amount may be debited to them immediately, rather than being saved for the next technical account. This can, in theory, result in a time saving of six months in reimbursing the Ceding Company for single large claim payments.

Reinsurers require a full refund of the cash loss payment to be reflected in the next technical account, whilst at the same time, the claim amount should appear within the paid losses item of the same account. This may seem like a complete waste of time, given that, usually, the cash loss refund is simply a corresponding and opposite entry to the amount included in the paid losses item. In other words, the two amounts cancel each other in the technical account. This is basically a London Market practice, which has existed for many years. It is designed in order to ensure that all transactions under the treaty are recorded somewhere within the technical accounts. It is a common cause of misunderstandings between London brokers and their overseas clients, and often leads to reconciliation problems, due to different ways of handling, as described in the following example.

On 5 March, the Ceding Company pays a large claim. The share of the treaty reinsurers amounts to $1 million, and the Ceding Company requests a cash loss collection from its London broker. The broker contacts all of the reinsurers and within 10 days has collected $230,000 which it remits to the client. Over the next two weeks, the broker collects further amounts of $10,000, $3,400 and $12,800 on various dates, which it remits periodically to the Ceding Company. The Ceding Company prepares its account on 31 March and includes the full amount of the cash loss within the paid losses. Some time later, the Ceding Company pays the balance of the technical account to the broker, and in doing so, refunds any cash loss payments it has received. This seems totally logical to the Ceding Company, because it cannot see the sense in returning any moneys it has not received!

The problems arise in the broker's books, because:

1. The London Market requires that a full cash loss refund should be shown in the next technical account after the cash call. Invariably, the broker will attempt to comply, by adjusting the technical account.
2. Some payments made by the broker may not have been received or reconciled by the Ceding Company at the time the latter settles his fiduciary account to the broker.

3. The broker may find it hard to identify which reinsurers' payments are being refunded.

Whilst many overseas ceding companies are baffled by the logic of the London Market way of handling cash losses, they should have nothing to fear from it. In effect, the claims entry and the refund cancel each other out, leaving the original cash loss call still to be collected from any late paying reinsurers. Having said that, brokers should also remember that they are providers of a service, and that they should adapt their service to the needs of their clients, rather than the other way round.

PREMIUM AND LOSS PORTFOLIO TRANSFERS

In order to understand this concept we must first examine the method of accounting which makes it necessary. There are two basic methods of accounting under a proportional treaty (see Figures 3 and 4):

1. Underwriting Year basis;
2. "Clean Cut" basis.

Underwriting Year basis

Traditionally, proportional treaties have been regarded as continuous contracts, with a specified anniversary date. The annual periods between anniversary dates are known as "underwriting years".

If, for example, a treaty is arranged so that each underwriting year runs from 1 January to 31 December, all policies which commence between those dates will belong to that particular underwriting year. Therefore it is quite possible that a policy could be issued on 30 December 1995 and would still be in force on 29 December 1996 (in fact, some classes of business, such as Contractors' All Risks, may have policy periods spanning many years). All premium and claims transactions on original policies are deemed to belong to the underwriting year in which the individual policies commenced, irrespective of when the actual transaction takes place.

In the example in Figure 3, an original policy, of 12 months' duration, commenced during the 1994 underwriting year. The premium would probably be accounted to reinsurers in the third quarterly account of 1994. Although the loss occurs in 1995, the settlement process could take several months, and final settlement might not occur until some time during 1996. In this case, as the claim is settled in April 1996, it would probably be debited to the reinsurers in the second quarter of 1996. On an underwriting year basis, however, all transactions relating to policies commencing during an underwriting year must be separately identifiable from the transactions of policies starting in other years. In other words, if the treaty commences in 1994, there will be four

Figure 3: Underwriting Year basis

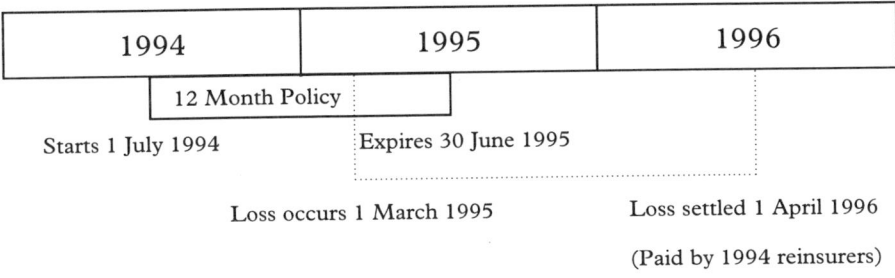

quarterly accounts issued in 1994. In 1995 there could be eight quarterly accounts; four applying to the 1994 underwriting year and four for 1995. Similarly, in 1996, there could be 12 quarterly accounts. In fact, there will continue to be accounts issued in respect of the 1994 underwriting year for as long as there are any financial transactions on policies which commenced during 1994. Considering the length of time which some claims take to be settled, there can be a great number of accounts for each underwriting year, and this can create a great administrative burden.

"Clean Cut" basis

For treaties covering certain types of business, there is an alternative accounting method, which is far easier to administer. This is known as the "Clean Cut" method.

In the example in Figure 4 overleaf, all policy periods which are still running beyond the anniversary date of the treaty are effectively cancelled and re-underwritten into the next treaty year. The reinsurers of the "old" year give back a portion of the premiums representing the unexpired periods of all policies ceded to the treaty. The "new" reinsurers would receive these "unexpired premiums" and would then be responsible for any new claims which occur. Similarly, if there are any claims which are outstanding at the anniversary date of the treaty, these will be paid by the "old" reinsurers to the "new" reinsurers, who will then reimburse the Ceding Company, as and when the individual claims are settled.

This exercise is known as *portfolio transfer*, and a treaty which is subject to an annual portfolio transfer of both unexpired premiums and outstanding claims is known as a *Clean Cut Treaty*.

Figure 4: "Clean Cut" basis

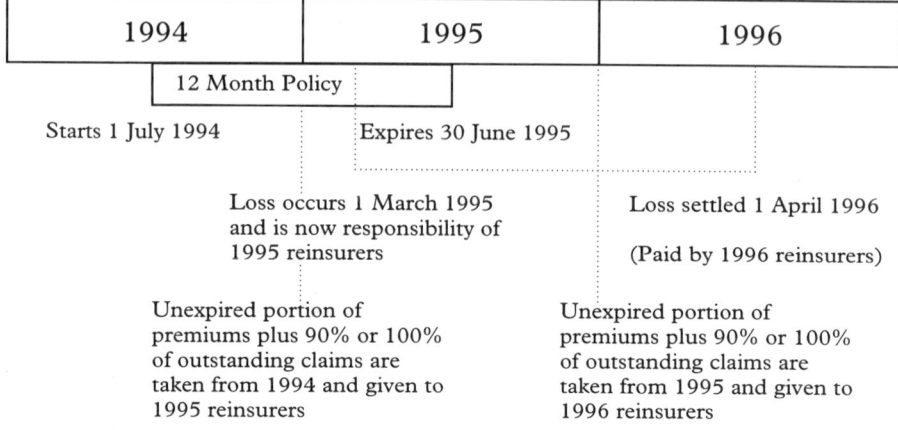

CALCULATION OF UNEXPIRED PREMIUMS

In a perfect world, it should be easy to calculate on a daily pro-rata basis the exact amount of premium for the unexpired portion of every ceded policy at a given date. For example, if the treaty year runs from 1 January, any ceded policy which begins on that date (and runs for 12 months) will expire on 31 December. There will therefore be no unexpired premiums on such policies.

Similarly, policies which commence on 2 January will not expire until the day after the end of the treaty year. In other words, 1/365th of the premiums from such policies will be unexpired. If we wanted to transfer the unexpired portion of those policies to a new group of reinsurers, we would need to take 1/365th of the premiums from the "old" reinsurers and give it to the "new" reinsurers, who would then become responsible for any claims which occurred on the last day of the policy period.

It should be relatively straightforward to perform a similar calculation for every policy which is ceded to the treaty, to arrive at a fair amount of premium to represent the unexpired policy periods. However, in the days before the widespread use of computers this was a cumbersome exercise, and complications can arise when there are some policies with periods of more or less than one year, or when some policies are amended in mid-period, in such a way that there are premium alterations.

If some method can be employed which would make the calculation of the unexpired premiums much easier, any slight inaccuracies produced by such a method would be more than compensated by its time savings, compared with the complicated daily pro-rata calculation.

The 1/24ths system

The earliest attempt to simplify the unexpired premium calculation was the 1/24ths system. This uses the assumption that all policies which commence in a particular month will have an *average* commencement date of the middle day of the month. So, for example, all policies which commence during January are taken as having an inception date of 16 January. At the end of December, these policies will *on average* have a half of one month still to run. In other words, the unexpired premiums from all January's policies will be 1/24th of the total premiums on policies starting in January ($1/2 \times 1/12$). The February policies will all be assumed to have started on 14 February, and therefore at the end of December these policies will have one and a half months still to run. One month is 1/12 of a year, and 1/2 of a month is 1/24th of a year, so the unexpired premiums for the February policies is taken as 3/24ths of the February premiums.

It is easy to perform these calculations on the premiums of every month, ending with December, in which 23/24ths of the premiums are taken as unexpired. The unexpired premiums for each month are then totalled, treaty commission and tax is deducted, and the resulting amount is taken away from the "old" reinsurers, and given to the "new" reinsurers.

Note that the *premium portfolio withdrawal* is made net of commission and taxes at the commission rate applicable to the "old" year, even if the commission rate changes from one year to the next. This is a market convention, because commission rates may go up or down between treaty years, and it is therefore necessary to standardise a procedure so that the effects of such fluctuations cancel each other out. There is a very good reason why premium portfolio transfers are made on a net basis, rather than based on gross premiums. The commission which reinsurers pay to the Ceding Company is partly a reimbursement for the expenses incurred by the Ceding Company in underwriting the business. The Ceding Company is normally competing for business in a local market, and quite often much of the original business comes from brokers or agents. The local brokers are free to use any licensed insurance company in the market, and will direct their clients to the company which will pay them the best commission. The Ceding Company must therefore know, at the beginning of the year, how much commission it can pay to its brokers and agents for any particular class of business. As the Ceding Company will be paying the brokers a fixed rate of commission on each policy, he cannot afford the uncertainty of potentially having to bear a reduction in treaty commission in the next treaty year, and having, in effect, to refund some of the treaty commission on the unexpired liabilities. In other words, treaty commission levels are an important part of the budget process for the business plan of the *whole underwriting year*.

1/8ths system

The 1/8ths system is a development of the thought process which came up with the 1/24ths system. If we accept that the potential for inaccuracy in the 1/24ths system is more than offset by the administrative savings, we are beginning to move away from the concept of proportional reinsurance being an exact science, and towards the idea that "near enough is good enough".

Therefore, if it is reasonable to assume that all policies starting in a particular month will have an average starting date in the middle of the month, we can reasonably extend the logic to say that all policies starting in a three-month period (or *quarter*) will have an average starting date in the middle of the quarter. In other words, business starting in the first quarter of the year will have an unexpired portion at the end of the year equivalent to a half of the quarter's premiums. A half of one quarter is 1/8th and so we can assume that 1/8th of the first quarter's premiums will be unexpired at the end of the year. Business which starts in the second quarter will be assumed to expire midway through the second quarter of the following year. Therefore at the end of the year, one-and-a-half quarters of the second quarter policy premiums will be unearned. One-and-a-half quarters is expressed as 3/8ths. The third quarter will have 5/8ths unexpired at the end of the year, and the fourth quarter will have 7/8ths.

Again, the quarterly unexpired premiums will be totalled at the end of the year. Commission and taxes will be deducted at the rate applicable to the old year, and the resulting amount will be taken from the "old" reinsurers and given to the "new" reinsurers. Often, there is no change to the panel of reinsurers from one year to the next, and so the *portfolio withdrawal* and the *portfolio entry* are for identical amounts, and are merely a *book entry*.

A fixed percentage

Having made a leap of faith with the 1/24ths system, and a further one with the 1/8ths system, why not go further? We could assume that all policies which start in a given year will have an average inception date in the middle of the year, and that, at the end of the year, roughly 50 per cent of the written premiums will be unexpired. Bearing in mind that premium portfolio transfers are made net of commission, we can arrive at a net figure, simply by deducting the commission percentage from 50 per cent of the year's premium. For example, if the commission for the treaty is set at 40 per cent, then 50 per cent less 40 per cent of 50 per cent comes to 30 per cent and we could therefore withdraw 30 per cent of the year's gross premiums from the old reinsurers, and pass the same amount to the new reinsurers who would then take on the unexpired policy periods.

In practice, commissions vary between treaties, and some reinsurers like to take into account any bias in the original business. For example, some companies might renew a large portion of their policies on 31 December, whilst

Calculation of Unexpired Premiums 39

others might renew more on 1 January. If the treaty year runs from 1 January to 31 December, having a large number of policies starting on 1 January would mean that the unexpired premiums in real terms would be much less than 50 per cent. Conversely, if large numbers of policies begin on 31 December, the unexpired premium figure could be much higher. Figures of between 30 and 45 per cent are commonly used in treaties these days, and once agreed upon, the figure is rarely ever changed, even if the treaty commission changes from one year to the next.

The 1/24ths and 1/8ths systems are still in use, although the flat percentage is now much more popular.

There are certain questions which frequently arise with regard to the operation of portfolio transfers, such as the following.

What if the Quota Share percentage changes?

A portfolio transfer is designed to transfer the unexpired liabilities from one group of reinsurers to another. When a Ceding Company has a Quota Share Treaty, it takes a percentage for itself, known as the retention. Therefore, as far as the Quota Share Treaty is concerned, the Ceding Company is just another reinsurer. If the retention changes from 10 to 20 per cent between one year and the next, the Ceding Company will pay away 10 per cent of the outgoing portfolio amounts and will take back 20 per cent of the same 100 per cent amounts. After the portfolio transfer is completed, the Ceding Company will be liable for 20 per cent of all amounts due from the Quota Share Treaty, even though at the time some of the original policies were underwritten, the Ceding Company only had a 10 per cent share. It can be deduced that the Ceding Company can make a short term improvement in its cash flow position by increasing its retention, especially if there are some large outstanding losses at the time the portfolio transfer is made. Nevertheless, it would be foolish to increase the retention beyond safe limits, simply to obtain some short term finance.

What if a reinsurer's share changes?

In exactly the same way, a reinsurer's share may change from one year to the next. The reinsurer may benefit in the short term by having a larger share of the incoming portfolio than the outgoing. The converse is equally true.

What if treaty limits increase/reduce?

Increasing the limit of a treaty does not usually affect the portfolio transfer in any way. For example, if the treaty limit increases from £10 million to £15 million, the incoming portfolio will still be based on the old treaty limits. The problem occurs when the treaty limits are reduced. If reinsurers are accepting a treaty with a limit of £10 million, they may not be happy to receive an incoming portfolio of business with a maximum limit of £15 million. Unless the Ceding Company is able to recalculate each individual cession (and find reinsurance for any unexpired risks which are surplus to the new treaty limits) or the reinsurers are prepared specially to agree to the incoming portfolio at the higher limits, the portfolio transfer should be waived for that year, and the unexpired liabilities of the old year should be allowed to run off naturally.

What if the treaty is cancelled?

If the treaty is cancelled, there is obviously nowhere to transfer the unexpired liabilities into. In such circumstances it is usual to allow the last treaty year to run off. In other words, the reinsurers on the last treaty year will remain liable until all policies have expired and all losses have been settled. This can take several years, and sometimes the Ceding Company will wait until all policies have expired and most of the larger claims have been settled, before offering reinsurers a final cut off, in exchange for reinsurers paying a percentage of the outstanding losses.

How are portfolio transfers affected by premium and loss reserves?

If a Ceding Company is legally required, or contractually entitled to retain reserves, it stands to reason that the operation of the portfolio transfer provisions should not be allowed to diminish the amount of reserve which the Ceding Company is holding. On the other hand, the expiring reinsurers are being released from all further liability, and are therefore entitled to receive a return of all reserves which have been withheld from them, plus any accrued interest.

For example, if the treaty is accounted quarterly, and reserves generate interest at an annual rate of 4 per cent, at the end of the year the first quarter's premium reserve will have been withheld for three quarters. It should be refunded to the reinsurer with 3 per cent interest. The amount of the first quarter's reserve should be withheld from the new reinsurers, out of the incoming premium portfolio amount, and released at the end of the first quarter of the new treaty year with 1 per cent interest. Similarly, the second quarter's premium reserve will have been withheld for two quarters at the time of transfer, and the old year's reinsurers will be entitled to 2 per cent interest, whilst the new reinsurers will have the premium reserve amount withheld until the end of the second quarter, when they will receive 2 per cent interest.

Profit commission

A profit commission is a payment made by the reinsurers to the Ceding Company as a reward for profitable underwriting. It is paid in accordance with an agreed formula, such as:

Profit commission: 25% (5% reinsurers' expenses, deficit carried forward to extinction).

In the above example, 25 per cent of the profit for the year is rebated to the Ceding Company, but how is the profit for the year actually calculated? Logic tells us that "profit" is the amount by which income exceeds outgo, but we need to know which of the various financial transactions to consider within the calculation.

Income

The only obvious item of income is the total amount of premium ceded to the treaty, net of any return premiums. Indeed, if all liabilities for the treaty year have expired before any profit commission calculation is performed, this is the only item of income relevant to the calculation. However, things are rarely that simple. As we have seen, the life of a proportional treaty extends a long way beyond the end of its underwriting year, unless special clean-cutting arrangements are made which determine the manner in which past and future liabilities are dealt with. Profit commission calculations can be highly complex affairs, depending upon how these matters are dealt with.

For our first example, we shall take a clean cut fire treaty in its first year of operation. The main characteristics of the treaty are as follows:

Commission:	35%
Premium portfolio:	40% of gross ceded premiums
Loss portfolio:	90% of outstanding losses
Profit commission:	25% (5% reinsurers' expenses. Deficit carried forward to extinction).

At the end of the treaty year, the relevant figures are as follows:

Premiums ceded:	348,540
Paid losses:	124,678
Outstanding losses:	103,154

The profit commission statement would look like this:

Income

Premiums ceded: 348,540

Outgo

Commission at 35%	121,989
Paid losses:	124,678
Premium portfolio withdrawal at 40%	139,436
Outstanding loss withdrawal at 90%	92,839
Reinsurers' expenses at 5%	17,427

Total of outgo	496,369
Income	348,540
Deficit	147,829

The item "reinsurers' expenses" is a factor which reinsurers build into the profit commission calculation to compensate for the brokerage and other expenses they have incurred in obtaining and handling the treaty. It is a way of ensuring that profit commission is not paid on the entire premium. Looking at it another way, if we imagine that without this "fictitious" item of outgo, the balance of the above calculation would be exactly zero, the reinsurers are technically in a break even situation, whereas in reality, they would be making a loss, due to the brokerage and other costs they have incurred in handling the business. Therefore, if the overall balance, without deducting reinsurers' expenses, were a small profit, reinsurers could be liable to pay a profit commission even though they themselves have not made any profit.

It stands to reason that the higher the reinsurers' expenses percentage, the less profit commission will be paid. It is therefore in the Ceding Company's interest to fix this figure as low as possible.

We can see that this particular year of the treaty is in deficit, as far as that profit commission calculation is concerned. However, much of the deficit has been brought about by the fact that there were premium and loss portfolio withdrawals at the end of the year, but there were no portfolio entries at the beginning of the year, because this was the first year of the treaty. The portfolio withdrawals were made in order to relieve the present reinsurers of future liabilities, and correspondingly, the profit commission calculation was based upon these "finally" determined figures.

In the following year, we assume that the financial provisions of the treaty are unchanged, and that the trading figures are as follows:

Premiums ceded:	347,928
Paid losses:	134,759
Outstanding losses:	95,784

Note that the paid and outstanding losses include any amounts paid during the current year or still outstanding, even if the losses happened during the previous year. Similarly, the premium figure includes any premiums on last year's policies which have been accounted this year.

The profit commission calculation for this year would be as follows:

Income

Premiums ceded:	347,928
Premium portfolio entry at 40%	139,436
Outstanding loss entry at 90%	92,839
Total of income:	580,203

Calculation of Unexpired Premiums

Outgo

Commission at 35%	121,775
Paid losses:	134,759
Premium portfolio withdrawal at 40%	139,171
Outstanding loss withdrawal at 90%	86,206
Reinsurers' expenses at 5%	17,396
Total of outgo	499,307
Income	580,203
Profit for year:	80,986
Deficit c/f from previous year	147,829
Final deficit:	66,933

As we can see, the deficit from the previous year has been brought into the calculation, turning an otherwise profitable year into a deficit for the purpose of the profit commission calculation. As the deficit is to be carried forward to extinction, the figure of 66,933 should be carried forward into next year's profit commission calculation and so on, until the calculation results in a profit, at which time 25 per cent of the profit will be paid by the reinsurers to the Ceding Company.

PRACTICAL EXERCISES 2(A) AND (B): PROFIT COMMISSION CALCULATIONS

(a) Calculate the profit commission for the third year, if the figures at the end of that year are as follows:

Premiums ceded:	428,394
Losses paid:	104,346
Outstanding losses:	65,987

(b) Calculate the profit commission for the last three years, using the same figures, but taking 7.5 per cent as reinsurers' expenses, instead of 5 per cent. (See Appendix 2 for answers to Practical Exercises 2(a) and (b).)

Deficit carry forward

Often reinsurers will not insist that deficits are carried forward until they have been extinguished (cancelled out by profitable results), but will specify a maximum period, after which time the deficit will be ignored. Hence, instead of seeing "Deficits carried forward to extinction", we may see "Deficits carried forward three years". In such cases, it is important when compiling a profit commission statement, to show any past deficits separately, clearly identifying the year such deficit was incurred, so that it can be ignored after its specified time period has expired.

Underwriting year basis

As you can see, the calculation of a profit commission is fairly straightforward when the treaty is accounted on an annual clean cut basis. However, many treaties operate on an underwriting year basis, and this is where profit commission calculations may become hugely complicated.

As an example, let us look at a Fire Treaty which operates on an underwriting year basis. The profit commission calculation might comprise the following elements:

Income

Premiums ceded during the year under review.
Premium reserve brought forward from the previous year.
Outstanding losses brought forward from the previous year.

Outgo

Commissions and taxes.
Five per cent of the ceded premiums as reinsurers' expenses.
Premium reserve at 40 per cent of ceded premiums.
Losses and loss expenses paid.
Outstanding losses at the effective date of the profit commission calculation.
Deficit carried forward from any previous underwriting year, for a maximum of three years.

It is usually stated in the treaty wording that the second two items of income shall not apply to the first profit commission calculation of any underwriting year, and that the last item of outgo shall not apply to the first underwriting year of the treaty. However, most wordings leave us to guess at the practicalities of the actual calculation, and the following will hopefully clarify the situation.

Let us assume that we are dealing with a completely new treaty. The first anniversary date has arrived and it is time to prepare the first profit commission statement. As this is both the first year of the treaty, and the first profit commission calculation of the underwriting year, we can ignore the last two items of income as well as the last item of outgo. The profit commission calculation is therefore similar to a clean cut treaty, as follows:

Income

Premiums ceded:	348,540

Outgo

Commission at 35%	121,989
Paid losses:	124,678
Premium reserve at 40%	139,436
Outstanding losses at 100%	103,154
Reinsurers' expenses at 5%	17,427

Calculation of Unexpired Premiums 45

Total of outgo	506,684
Income	348,540
Deficit	158,144

Twelve months later, there are two things to do. We need to prepare a second profit commission statement for the first underwriting year, as well as a first statement for the second underwriting year.

The second statement for the first underwriting year would now include the last two items of income, because we are updating last year's figures, and so it might look like this:

Income

Premiums ceded:	246,156
Premium reserve brought forward	139,436
Outstanding losses brought forward	103,154
Total of income	488,746

Outgo

Commission at 35%	86,155
Paid losses:	84,734
Premium reserve at 40%	139,171
Outstanding losses at 100%	42,106
Reinsurers' expenses at 5%	12,308
Total of outgo	364,474
Income	488,746
Profit for year:	124,272
Previous deficit	− 158,144
Deficit for underwriting year	− 33,872

When preparing the first profit commission statement of the second underwriting year, we must carry forward the deficit figure of 33,872 and keep carrying it forward into the profit commission calculations of subsequent underwriting years, either until it is cancelled out by profits, or until it is effectively "time barred" by the carry forward limitation of three or five years.

Please note that in order to operate this time bar, it is necessary to omit the deficit from the main body of the income/outgo calculation in order to arrive at the pure situation for the underwriting year, and then to show any deficits carried forward underneath, separately for each underwriting year. In this way, it will be easy to see whether earlier years' deficits are being reduced or eliminated by the profits of subsequent years, as well as whether the carry forward period has expired. The problem with the calculation formula as contained in many wordings is that if you do exactly as the formula says, and incorporate any previous years' deficits as an item of outgo, you will never be able to identify separately which underwriting year any deficits relate to, and could end up carrying forward the deficits to extinction.

It stands to reason that in the third year, we still need to adjust the profit commission of the first underwriting year, as well as adjusting the second year's profit commission and preparing a brand new one for the third underwriting year. It also follows that the deficit which you carried forward from the first underwriting year to the second will probably have changed. This will go on until all liabilities of some of the earlier years are finalised. It would be unnecessarily prolix to carry on with the examples, but needless to say, this kind of system, although common, can prove to be an administrative nightmare.

Of course, the deficit carry forward provisions can lead to further complications, such as the following.

What happens if we have a Quota Share Treaty, and the retention changes?

Actually, this is an easy one. If you imagine the profit commission calculation as being done in 100 per cent terms, i.e. including the retention, the Ceding Company is just like any other reinsurer. If they take an increased retention, say from 40 per cent one year to 50 per cent the next year, the same 100 per cent figure is being carried forward as a deficit, but the Ceding Company is only collecting 50 per cent profit commission instead of 60 per cent.

What happens if the shares of individual reinsurers change?

This is a very interesting question. Strictly speaking, the Ceding Company is entering into separate reinsurance agreements with every single one of its reinsurers, and is therefore entitled to prepare a separate profit commission statement for each of them, bringing forward the precise monetary amount of deficit which each reinsurer has incurred in previous years. In other words, a Ceding Company could, in theory, sustain a large loss one year, change all its treaty reinsurers the next year, and not give them the benefit of any deficit brought forward (because, as new reinsurers, they did not sustain the deficit).

In practice, most Ceding Companies are happy to prepare their profit commission statements on a 100 per cent basis, ignoring the potential for gaining small amounts of profit commission at the expense of a huge workload. It should be said also, that some reinsurers can take advantage of this situation by coming onto a treaty after there has been a major loss, thereby avoiding having to pay profit commission for a number of years.

Some treaties, particularly covering Contractors All Risks business, specify that the first profit commission statement of each underwriting year may only be calculated at the end of the third accounting year. This is because the business typically ceded to such treaties consists of policies of a long term nature, such as building projects lasting several years. It is argued that there is no point in trying to calculate the profit of an underwriting year until most of its business has expired.

Calculation of Unexpired Premiums

As with most matters in reinsurance, methods of calculation are infinitely variable, and a degree of common sense is required. It would be quite possible to write a whole book on the subject of profit commission alone.

One final point about profit commission concerns the confusing terminology. Many drafters of slips and wordings will insist on using the phrase "losses carried forward five years". This is highly confusing, because most people understand "losses" as synonymous with "claims". It is far clearer to use the word "deficits".

"Management expenses" means exactly the same as "reinsurers' expenses" and is an artificial outgo item, designed to make the profit look smaller, so that reinsurers do not pay a profit commission on the whole technical profit. This is because the technical profit is not a true profit for the reinsurer, as he must use some of it to pay the broker, as well as his own expenses. An amusing story concerns an underwriter who once refused a broker's request to increase the management expenses under a treaty, and insisted on reducing them!

CHAPTER 4

PROPORTIONAL TREATY WORDINGS AND CLAUSES

Like any complex financial arrangement, a reinsurance treaty requires documentary evidence of the contract. In direct insurance, we have the insurance policy, with which we are all familiar. In treaty reinsurance, the equivalent document is the "treaty wording" which details the scope of cover, the limits, the financial aspects and other issues, such as the procedures to be followed in the event of the insolvency of one of the contracting parties, the outbreak of war and other issues.

Of course, different classes of business have their own particular clauses and procedures, but most wordings follow a similar layout, as you will see from the specimens in Appendix 5.

The following clauses deserve special mention.

PERIOD AND TERMINATION

Most proportional treaties are regarded as having an indefinite duration, and may only be cancelled at certain dates (referred to as the "anniversary date" of the contract), by either party giving notice before a certain time. For example, if the anniversary date of a treaty is 31 December of any year, and the "notice period" is three months, any party wishing to cancel the contract will need to notify the other party before 30 September. If neither party tenders notice of cancellation before the deadline expires, the contract will continue in force until the next opportunity to cancel, which means that one of the parties will need to give notice before 30 September of the following year, to take effect on the following 31 December.

In practice, nearly all reinsurers give notice of cancellation to all of their Ceding Companies every year, in order to review statistical information, whether they intend to cancel or not. This practice is known as "issuing provisional notice of cancellation" (referred to commonly as "PNOC"), and is the cause of much ritual drudgery in every reinsurance broking house in London.

Actually, the word "provisional" has no legal force whatsoever. If one party gives notice of cancellation, then the treaty is under notice, and either party may regard the contract as terminated at the next anniversary date, unless both parties mutually agree otherwise.

The word "provisional" is used as some kind of polite statement of intent that the issuing party still wishes to consider continuing his involvement. Of course, the converse to this is when a party issues "definite notice of cancellation". By including the word "definite", the issuing party is giving the other party plenty of warning that another partner needs to be found.

However, in the contract wording there is no distinction between definite or provisional notice of cancellation; there is merely "notice of cancellation", the issuance of which will allow both parties the freedom to renegotiate or cancel the contract.

It is a common misconception that one party may issue notice of cancellation, giving him the right to do what he likes, but that if the other party wants to enjoy similar freedom of action, he must also give notice of cancellation. The wording invariably states that the contract "may be cancelled at the anniversary date by either party giving three months prior notice ...". In other words, notice of cancellation, provided it is given in the proper manner, as set out in the wording, means that the contract between the two parties will terminate at the next anniversary date. Any agreement made subsequently between the parties, even if they simply agree to carry on as before, effectively becomes a new contract. Of course, in all other ways, the contract will still be regarded as a continuation of the existing contract, for example for the purposes of maintaining the premium and loss reserve accounts or the deficit carry forward provisions of the profit commission calculation and so on.

It should be added that many companies, particularly in the London Market, when signing a slip, will endorse their lines with the letters "NCAD". This stands for "Notice of Cancellation at Anniversary Date" and means that the reinsurer is telling the Ceding Company that his participation is annual, and must be renegotiated every year. The broker must be careful to advise his client of all lines which are subject to this provision, either at the time he confirms cover, or before the annual deadline for tendering notice of cancellation.

Lloyd's syndicates do not mark their acceptances in this way, and there is in fact a difference in procedure between the Marine and Non-marine markets. The Non-marine markets require that the broker assumes that the lines are annual only. This is entirely sensible, as each syndicate only exists as a legal entity for one year, after which it is dissolved and reconstituted. Marine syndicates, on the other hand, prefer to issue their own notice of cancellation every year, and will be most upset with the broker if he gives notice of cancellation on behalf of a syndicate who has not instructed him to do so.

Most brokers clarify the situation by endorsing their slips with "Internal Arrangements" which state that the broker is entitled to give notice of cancellation on behalf of all Lloyd's syndicates at each anniversary date.

ERRORS AND OMISSIONS

This clause once featured in almost all treaty wordings, proportional or excess of loss. In recent years, however, there have been attempts to remove this clause from excess of loss covers. Its presence in proportional treaties is said to cater for inadvertent errors or omissions made by the Ceding Company when ceding risks. For example, the Ceding Company may have incorrectly classified the risk as being of first class construction, only to find later that the building was made of wood. The Ceding Company would be bound to rectify the error, but the fact that the error had been made could not be used by the reinsurer as an excuse for getting out of the contract. As excess of loss contracts do not take cessions of individual risks, but merely protect the Ceding Company against losses above a certain size, it is argued that the Errors and Omissions clause is not necessary.

However, many Ceding Companies feel safer with an "E & O" clause in all of their contracts, and some modified clauses have been introduced into excess of loss contracts, which allow for certain types of errors and omissions to be made without resulting in the avoidance of the contract.

SELF INSURED OBLIGATIONS

This clause basically allows the Ceding Company to insure itself, and to cede these insurances to the treaty as if they were any other policy. When a company insures itself, it has no legal liability to itself under the policy. Nevertheless, many insurance companies insure, for example, their own office buildings, and wish to reinsure part of the risk in the same way as they reinsure their other risks. Some reinsurers do not like this clause, because they fear that it could lead to abuses. For example, the company might charge itself a very low premium, or be very liberal with itself in the adjustment of claims. This is a very strange fear for reinsurers to have. After all, a reinsurance treaty is the ultimate display of good faith which a reinsurer can show to a Ceding Company. It therefore seems odd that, having put so much faith in the Ceding Company, the reinsurer should have cause to doubt the integrity of the Ceding Company in the matter of its own insurances.

INSPECTION OF RECORDS

A reinsurance treaty is a contract of utmost good faith, in exactly the same way as any other insurance contract. In fact, a treaty is often an act of blind faith because the reinsurer rarely ever comes into contact with the details of individual risks which are ceded to him under the treaty. The reinsurer puts his faith in the management of the reinsured company, in particular the company's underwriters and underwriting philosophy.

Sometimes, however, reinsurers require a little more reassurance that all is well, and may wish to conduct an inspection of the Reinsured's books. The inspection may be aimed at gathering evidence for a dispute between the reinsurer and the Reinsured. Fortunately, such disputes are rare, and the more usual reason for an inspection is for the reinsurer to satisfy himself that the company's underwriting procedures and internal controls are working properly. Such routine "audits" are becoming more common practice among some of the larger reinsurance companies, and can benefit the Reinsured by alerting him to any slipping of standards uncovered by the reinsurer.

There are a number of different clause wordings, but in broad terms they contain the following elements:

- The reinsurer has a right to inspect only the records of the Reinsured which relate to business falling under the treaty.
- The reinsurer must give reasonable notice to the Reinsured.
- The reinsurer may request copies of relevant documents, and may be required to meet the expense of copying.
- The reinsurer's inspection rights will survive the cancellation or expiry of the treaty, but only whilst there are any outstanding liabilities.
- The reinsurer cannot use the inspection to delay settlement of any amounts due from him to the Reinsured.

Naturally, reinsurers are bound by the rules of confidentiality, and cannot use the information gleaned from the inspection, or any confidential information acquired through any other means, in any other context or in its dealings with any other company.

ARBITRATION

This is often the longest clause in a treaty wording, and is probably the least read for that very reason. When the reinsurer and the Reinsured fail to agree on the way the treaty should operate, arbitration is the usual remedy. Arbitration is chosen before legal action because:

- it is cheaper;
- it is quicker;
- the arbitrators are insurance experts.

Usually each party nominates one arbitrator, and the two arbitrators nominate an umpire. If the two arbitrators cannot agree between them, the umpire has the casting vote. The decision of the arbitration panel is final, and the panel also decides on the apportionment of the cost of the arbitration.

Once the arbitration panel has delivered its decision, any award made may be enforceable by the courts.

In recent years, it has been argued that the arbitration clause should be a separate agreement from the main treaty wording. This is because the clause constitutes an agreement to deal in a certain way with issues concerning the interpretation of the treaty. Arbitration could result in the setting aside of the treaty, which would then lead to a circular argument that if the treaty is no longer in force, how can an integral part of the treaty (the Arbitration clause) have any validity?

BORDEREAUX

This is not a wine growing region of France, but a list of all individual cessions to a proportional treaty. There are also claims bordereaux and outstanding claims bordereaux which, unsurprisingly, are lists of paid claims and outstanding claims under the treaty.

Back in the early days of treaties, when a treaty was not much more than a facultative facility, Reinsureds were expected to submit quarterly or even monthly bordereaux to their reinsurers, giving details of every risk ceded to the treaty, including the name of the insured, the policy number, as well as the sum insured and the policy premium, together with their respective distribution to the treaties.

These days it is rare for a treaty to contain a bordereau provision, but the same details are still kept by the Reinsured in the form of a cession register, which the reinsurers would be able to inspect under the terms of the Inspection of Records clause.

CHAPTER 5

DESIGNING A PROPERTY REINSURANCE PROGRAMME FROM HISTORICAL DATA

It is not very often that we design a reinsurance programme for a completely new company, where no statistical information exists.

All types of insurance yield statistical information from which projections can be made, but for the purpose of our first designing exercise we are going to take a look at a hypothetical property account.

We are given statistical information for the last five years in the form of a "Gross Account Risk Profile" which shows premiums, claims, numbers of risks and aggregate sums insured. This information is divided into bands according to the sum insured of each policy.

Our task is to discuss a suitable reinsurance programme based upon these figures.

There are several factors we need to consider.

Retention

The retention is the amount the company can afford to lose on a single risk or in a single event. As a general rule of thumb, this figure can be around 3 per cent of the company's paid up capital. A lower figure may be used by a new company, whilst an established company, with accumulated shareholders' funds, may increase this figure. Let us assume that for the purpose of this exercise, the company feels comfortable with a maximum retention of $250,000 per risk.

Table of limits

A proportional treaty is an obligatory reinsurance arrangement, under which the Reinsured makes cessions according to an agreed formula. The cession of any risk depends upon its size and characteristics.

A table of limits is often used as a way of "grading" risks according to construction and use. For example, an office block may be considered a very safe risk, and may be regarded as Class A occupancy. However, construction standards vary, and the Reinsured may have perhaps four construction standards, ranging from First Class (e.g. reinforced concrete) down to Fourth Class which would represent a poor type of construction, regarded as flammable. An

56 Designing a Property Reinsurance Programme

office building of First Class construction would therefore warrant a full retention of $250,000 in our example.

On the other hand, at the very bottom of the table we might find highly hazardous occupations, such as sawmills or paint manufacturers. A risk of this type may only merit a retention of 60 per cent of the Reinsured's normal maximum, and if the risk is of flammable construction, the figure may be as low as 30 per cent.

If at the time of underwriting, the Reinsured classifies each risk according to its occupancy and construction type, it should be a simple matter to produce future statistical information, broken down in a manner which will allow reliable projections to be made concerning the effects of different reinsurance programmes upon the net results of his portfolio. It would also allow the Reinsured and his reinsurers to determine whether the table of limits is a good one, or whether it should be altered in some way.

Table 4: A simplified table of limits

Construction/Occupancy	1	2	3	4
A	100%	90%	80%	70%
B	90%	80%	70%	60%
C	80%	70%	60%	50%
D	70%	60%	50%	40%
E	60%	50%	40%	30%

Having established the retention from the table of limits, the Reinsured should avoid the temptation to make arbitrary changes to it when ceding individual risks. In the first place, it is against the spirit of a reinsurance treaty agreement. Secondly, it makes analysis of the portfolio impossible if there is no formula for anticipating the likely effects of changes to the reinsurance programme. Sometimes the Reinsured will have good reason to alter his retention on a particular risk, in order to reduce exposures in a particular neighbourhood. The occasional deviation is allowable under treaty conditions, where it is considered to be in the reinsurers' interests, and should not have great consequences for the projection of treaty statistics. However, if the Reinsured is constantly altering retentions from those laid down in the table of limits, changes in underwriting policy are probably needed.

Results

The Reinsured is clearly looking to maximise his chance of making a profit. In this exercise we will regard the Reinsured's profit as:

Retained Premiums + Reinsurance Commission − retained losses − excess of loss reinsurance costs.

Of course there are many other factors in the profit equation, such as acquisition and administration costs, as well as the profit commission earned under treaties, and any differential between the rate of interest earned on retained premium reserves and the amount of agreed interest paid to the reinsurers. However, for our purposes these can be ignored, either because they are constant, or because their amounts are not usually significant.

Exposure

Assuming that the Reinsured is going to retain up to $250,000 on any one risk, there is virtually any number of ways to achieve this. For example, he may choose to retain up to $250,000 for his net account, and use proportional treaties for any amounts surplus to this figure. In the case of a risk worth $1 million he would keep 25 per cent for net account and cede 75 per cent to the treaty. He would give his reinsurers 75 per cent of the premium for that risk, and the reinsurers would in turn pay him 75 per cent of all losses which he incurs.

In the second example, the Reinsured decides to keep the first $1 million of each risk and protect himself against any losses which exceed $250,000 on any single risk (he arranges "per risk" excess of loss protection for $750,000 excess of $250,000).

On a risk with a sum insured of $1 million the Reinsured would not be ceding any of the premium to the proportional treaty, and would not therefore make any recoveries from the treaty if the risk were to be affected by a loss.

The difference between the above two methods can clearly be seen in the case of a $250,000 loss affecting the $1 million risk. Under the first example, the proportional treaty would pay 75 per cent of the loss, whereas under the second example, the proportional treaty would pay nothing. Also, as the Reinsured's net loss under the second example is only $250,000 there is no recovery from the per risk excess of loss programme.

Hence we can see that with proportional reinsurance, the Reinsured can recover a share of every loss, no matter how small. With excess of loss reinsurance, the Reinsured will only claim from his reinsurers when his claim exceeds the deductible. In other words, for the same retention of $250,000 the second example gives the Reinsured a considerably higher exposure than the first option. This exposure must be weighed up against the increase in retained premium and the cost of the risk excess of loss reinsurance.

Catastrophe

Taking the two examples mentioned above, the $1 million risk would contribute $250,000 to the Reinsured's aggregate retained exposures on the first basis, but a full $1 million on the second basis. Repeated over the entire portfolio, this could result in a significant increase in retained exposures. If the business is located in a part of the world which is prone to natural catastrophes or serious rioting, this exposure must be protected. Otherwise, the Reinsured could be wiped out by a series of losses arising out of one event. Obviously, if the Reinsured has more retained exposure, he will need to buy more catastrophe protection, and this will increase his costs.

Marketability

It is easily possible to design a reinsurance programme which will maximise the Reinsured's chance of making a profit. However, the converse is that such a programme could maximise the reinsurer's chance of making a loss.

Any responsible reinsurer wants to underwrite a profitable account, and we must therefore design a programme which will also be acceptable to the intended market.

Unfortunately, there are no rules to tell us precisely what is acceptable and what is not.

As an example, let us look at the question of *balance*. By this we mean the ratio of the cession limit per risk, against the estimated treaty premium income. If a treaty can accept up to $1 million of sum insured per risk and generates an overall premium income of $1 million per year, it is said to have a 1:1 balance.

There are no rules to say whether any particular balance is acceptable, because there are so many variables to consider. These variables include the normal level of profitability of the account, the territorial scope and its susceptibility to catastrophe perils, the class of business, the mix of the portfolio and so forth.

A 1:1 balance might be perfectly acceptable for a fire treaty in a part of the world which is not prone to natural disasters. On the other hand, in a seismically active region, this sort of balance would be unacceptable, because the profits of the good years would not be sufficient to allow reinsurers to build up a catastrophe reserve. Engineering treaties are treated differently still, and a 10:1 balance may even be considered acceptable by some markets.

DATA

The ideal set of data would comprise several years' figures for the Reinsured's gross account (i.e. before deducting any reinsurance premiums or claims). The figures would include the aggregate sums insured, premiums and claims, divided into bands of sum insured (or PML). Such *profiles* should be prepared separately for each section of the table of limits, so that we have one profile for all policies where the Reinsured normally retains 100 per cent of his maximum retention, another profile for policies where the retention would be 90 per cent of the maximum and so on. These profiles should be further broken down by catastrophe zone for parts of the world where natural catastrophe perils can occur.

It is clear that such an exercise can result in the generation of a huge amount of data. This may be beyond the scope of many companies to prepare, but with the increasing sophistication of database programmes, the possibilities for this sort of analysis are increasing.

For this exercise, we shall only concern ourselves with the estimation of retained premiums and reinsurance commissions, as well as the historical results of the retained portfolio and the treaties, based upon the chosen treaty structure. We must also consider the amount of retained aggregate under the chosen programme, and how much catastrophe reinsurance the company should purchase.

For the sake of this exercise, we shall assume that the results given below represent the average of the last five years results, loaded for inflation. We shall also assume that all risks in the portfolio are of Occupancy Class A and of First Class construction, located in a single catastrophe zone.

Table 5: Gross results of the portfolio

From	To	#	Aggregates	Premiums	Losses
1	100,000	500	25,000,000	39,252	41,250
100,001	200,000	381	56,350,251	102,870	92,480
200,001	300,000	221	53,168,324	68,524	59,389
300,001	500,000	141	54,289,132	63,450	51,250
500,001	750,000	98	67,543,200	86,724	43,267
750,001	1,000,000	78	64,254,678	67,894	36,589
1,000,001	2,000,000	63	92,345,876	104,987	74,567
2,000,001	3,000,000	24	62,347,865	65,476	36,890
3,000,001	5,000,000	12	49,785,765	51,378	24,321
5,000,001	10,000,000	4	34,567,432	36,578	0
10,000,001	20,000,000	3	48,097,865	49,876	0

The first two columns of Table 5 represent the minimum and maximum sums insured for each band. Hence any policy with a sum insured of $50,000 would appear in the first band. "#" represents the number of policies with sums insured falling within that band. "Aggregates" represent the total of the sums insured for all policies within that sum insured band, whilst the premium and loss figures are the total amounts for the underwriting year, applicable to the policies counted within that band.

Remember that some policies can cover several different risks, such as different locations for the same manufacturer etc. In most cases, cessions to treaties are made on the basis of the sum insured of the highest valued individual risk. For example, a policy may cover 10 locations, with the largest valued at $1.5 million. This policy would be ceded to the treaty based upon this sum insured, even though the total value of all of the locations may be $5 million. In the profile in Table 5, the policy would be shown in the band $1,000,001–$2 million and the entire policy premium, as well as the total of the sums insured for all of the locations would be put into that band. (Profiles for excess of loss covers should be prepared by individual location, if possible, for reasons which will be discussed later.)

APPORTIONMENT OVER THE TREATY PROGRAMME

This exercise, like most in reinsurance, is a question of best guessing. We are trying to estimate how the premiums, claims and aggregate sums insured would be apportioned over different types of reinsurance programme. In order to do this, we must make certain assumptions, the first of which is that every policy within each band has a sum insured equal to the mid-point of the band.

For example, in the band of sums insured between $1 million to $2 million the mid-point is roughly $1.5 million. If we are assuming that the Reinsured is going to retain the first $250,000 of sum insured on each risk, we can say that, for this band of the profile, the Reinsured would keep 250,000/1,500,000ths of the premiums, aggregate sums insured and claims. It is then a simple matter of applying the same principle to all bands of the profile and adding up the results. If the Reinsured prepares another profile of risks in Construction/Occupancy Group A2 (or B1), where the retention is 90 per cent of the maximum, a corresponding calculation would be done by applying the fraction 225,000/1,500,000ths and so on.

Following on from this, we would want to calculate the fraction of each band which would be allocated to the various treaties. Going back to the $250,000 retention and the $1,000,001–$2 million band, if we assume that the first 250,000 of each risk is retained, there is going to be $1.25 million of sum insured, per risk, left over, which equates to five times the retention. If we are looking at a first surplus treaty of five lines or more, we can allocate all of the remaining premiums, claims and aggregates to the treaty. On the other hand, if our hypothetical treaty only accepts up to four lines, then we must apply the fraction $1,000,000/$1,500,000 to the figures in the band. The remainder, after subtracting the amounts allocated to the retention and first surplus treaty, would go to the second surplus treaty, if there is one; otherwise it may be placed under a Facultative Obligatory Treaty or as a facultative reinsurance in the open market.

One final thing to mention, before we start to build a spreadsheet model, is the Quota Share Treaty. If, instead of taking a simple retention of the first

$250,000 of sum insured on each risk, we take up to $500,000 each risk, we can protect this with a 50 per cent Quota Share Treaty. This would alter the amount of each band which goes to the retention. In our example, we are now looking at a fraction of 50 per cent of 500,000/1,500,000ths. Taking $500,000 as the Gross Line, you can see that there are now two Gross Lines remaining, which would be allocated to the first surplus.

CONSTRUCTING THE SPREADSHEET

This model has been designed using Lotus 1-2-3, but can easily be converted to other spreadsheet formats.

First, we shall put in the profile. We shall start putting the figures in column A, row 9. This will give us some room at the top for titles and column headings. Hence our figure for losses in the sum insured range 1–100,000 will appear in cell F9.

Row	A7	B7	C7	D7	E7	F7
8	FROM	TO	#	Aggregates	Premiums	Losses
9	1	100,000	500	25,000,000	39,252	41,250
10	100,001	200,000	381	56,350,251	102,870	92,480
11	200,001	300,000	221	53,168,324	68,524	59,389
12	300,001	500,000	141	54,289,132	63,450	51,250

The next thing we need to do is set up the cells in which we are going to put our treaty programme details, such as the retained line, the Quota Share percentage, and the number of lines for each surplus treaty. This example assumes a maximum of three surplus treaties, with anything remaining going to facultative reinsurance.

In cell B32 we shall place the retained amount (the first "line"), placing its label in cell A32. This may be regarded either as a Gross Line, or a Net Line, depending upon whether there is a Quota Share Treaty. With just this figure, we can work on the data, calculating the allocation of the aggregates, premiums and losses to the first Line. This example assumes a retained line of $250,000.

	A	B
32	Line	250,000

We need to set up three columns which will perform the allocation calculations, starting at column G. In other words, column G9 will calculate the share of the aggregates (from D9) which falls to the first Line, H9 will calculate the share of the premium and K9 the losses.

	G	H	I
7		For 1st Line	
8	Aggregates	Premiums	Losses
9	[Formula, Cell G9]	Copy formula from G9	Copy formula from G9
10			
11			
12			

Here is the formula for cell G9:

@IF($B$32> = $B9,D9,$B$32/(($B9 + $A9)/2*D9)

For those who are not familiar with spreadsheets, let us examine the formula in detail. This formula is based on Boolean Algebra, which requires logical operators, such as IF, =, >, <, THEN and so on. In Lotus 1-2-3, such expressions start with the @ sign, followed by IF and an open bracket. A comma can mean either THEN or OTHERWISE, depending upon its placement in the equation. Each equation should have two commas, meaning THEN and OTHERWISE, in that order. The equation is then closed with a bracket.

The above equation, in English means:

"IF the amount of the first line of retention (cell B32) is greater than or equal to the highest sum insured in the range (cell B9), THEN put the whole aggregate figure from cell D9. OTHERWISE, take the amount of the first line of retention and divide it by half of the sum of the highest and lowest sums insured of the range (the mid-point) and multiply the result by the aggregate figure."

In spreadsheet programmes, if we were to copy our G9 formula into cell H9, the value D9 would automatically be corrected to E9, so that the formula would calculate based upon the premium for the band. Similarly, if we were to copy the formula from G9 into G10, any cell numbers would be increased by one. This is fine, provided that all of the data in the formula move across or up and down in the same way as the cell containing the formula. However, some of the data is static, in either one or both directions. In order to deal with this, we need to fix some of the cells in the formula, so that either or both of the column letters or row numbers do not get changed as we copy the formula to different cells.

We can do this in Lotus using the $ sign. If we want to anchor the column letter, we put a $ sign in front of it. If we want to anchor the row number, we put a $ sign before that. If we want to anchor both, we put $ signs in front of both. In the above example, cell B32 contains the value of the first line of retention. This will be a constant in the formula, so it has two $ signs. Columns B9 and A9 are only constant in one direction. When we copy the formula to cell H9, we still want the values of B9 and A9, but when we copy down to

G10, we want the values of cells B10 and A10. We do this by putting the $ sign only in front of the row number.

By writing the formula in this way, we can copy the formula into rows H and I and down through as many rows as we need.

The formula, when copied into the relevant cells of our model, will produce a result like this for a retention of $250,000:

Row No	G7 Aggregates	Line Premiums	I9 Losses
8			
9	25,000,000	39,252	41,250
10	56,350,251	102,870	92,480
11	53,168,218	68,524	59,389
12	33,930,665	39,656	32,031
13	27,017,258	34,690	17,307
14	18,358,469	19,398	10,454
15	15,390,974	17,498	12,428
16	6,234,785	6,548	3,689
17	3,111,610	3,211	1,520
18	1,152,248	1,219	0

Our next step is to calculate the shares of the various treaties, and for this we need some more data, showing the amount of the Quota Share Treaty (if any) and the number of Surplus Lines of each treaty. We are going to place a percentage figure for the Quota Share Treaty in cell E32. If the figure is zero, it means that there is no Quota Share Treaty, and the First Line figure in B32 is, in effect, a Net Line. If there is a figure, such as 70 per cent it means that there is 70 per cent Quota Share Treaty and that the Reinsured is retaining 30 per cent of all amounts calculated for the first Gross Line above. This figure will feature in the calculations later on, but for now, let us look at the calculations for a First Surplus Treaty.

For this, we need to know the number of lines of retention, either Gross or Net, which the treaty will accept. Let us use a figure of 4, which we will place in G32.

	F	G
32	1st Surplus No. of Lines:	4

We are going to calculate the Aggregate of the sums insured for row 9 in cell J9. The formula is as follows:

@IF(G9*($G$32+1)>D9,D9−G9,G9*$G$32)

64 Designing a Property Reinsurance Programme

In other words:

"IF the aggregates in G9 (the share to the first Line), multiplied by the number of lines plus 1 (being the first Line) are greater than 100 per cent aggregates, THEN put the 100 per cent aggregates minus the amount already allocated to the first Line. OTHERWISE, put the 100 per cent aggregates times the number of lines."

Note that we have anchored cell G32 in both directions, because the same value will be used when we copy the formula to columns K and L and down to row 18 (or further). The First Surplus allocations, after inserting the above formula, will look something like this:

	J	K	L
7		1st Surplus	
8	Aggregates	Premiums	Losses
9	0	0	0
10	0	0	0
11	106	0	0
12	20,358,467	23,794	19,219
13	40,525,942	52,034	25,960
14	45,896,209	48,496	26,135
15	61,563,897	69,991	49,711
16	24,939,141	26,190	14,756
17	12,446,440	12,844	6,080
18	4,608,991	4,877	0
19	3,206,524	3,325	0

For the Second Surplus Treaty, we are going to place the number of Lines at cell I32. We are then going to allocate the profile figures to this treaty in columns M, N and O.

	H	I
32	2nd Surplus No. of Lines:	2

The formula for cell M9 is as follows:

@IF(G9*($G$32 + $I$32 + 1)>D9,D9 − G9 − J9,G9*$I$32)

This means:

"IF the aggregates to the first Line, multiplied by the number of Lines of the First and Second Surplus Treaties plus one are greater than the 100 per cent aggregates, take the 100 per cent aggregates less the amounts to the first Line and the First Surplus Treaty. OTHERWISE, take the amount of aggregates to the first Line, multiplied by the number of Lines of the Second Surplus Treaty."

This formula can then be copied into columns N and O, and down through row 19 or more, which should give results like this for a two-line treaty:

	M	N	O
7		2nd Surplus	
8	Aggregates	Premiums	Losses
9	0	0	0
10	0	0	0
11	0	0	0
12	0	0	0
13	0	0	0
14	0	0	0
15	15,391,005	17,498	12,428
16	12,469,571	13,095	7,378
17	6,223,220	6,422	3,040
18	2,304,495	2,439	0
19	1,603,262	1,663	0

For the Third Surplus Treaty, we need a number of Lines, which we shall place in cell K32.

	J	K
32	3rd Surplus No. of Lines	3

The aggregates, premiums and losses will be calculated in columns P, Q, and R. The formula to calculate the aggregates for cell P9 is as follows:

@IF(G9*($G$32 + $I$32 + $K$32 + 1)>D9,D9 − G9 − J9 − M9,G9*$K$32)

By now, you should be following the sequence, and should not need an explanation of this formula. Needless to say, this formula can be copied into columns Q and R, as well as down through to row 19 or more.

The results, using an example of a three-line treaty, would be as follows:

	P	Q	R
7		3rd Surplus	
8	Aggregates	Premiums	Losses
9	0	0	0
10	0	0	0
11	0	0	0

	P	Q	R
12	0	0	0
13	0	0	0
14	0	0	0
15	0	0	0
16	18,704,356	19,643	11,067
17	9,334,830	9,633	4,560
18	3,456,743	3,658	0
19	2,404,893	2,494	0

Next, we want to calculate anything left over, after allocations to the retention and all treaties. We shall assume that these amounts, which should only represent a small number of large risks, are placed facultatively, or to a Facultative Obligatory Treaty. We are therefore going to calculate values for columns S, T and U. This is the easy part, as shown in the formula for cell S9:

+ D9 − G9 − J9 − M9 − P9

In other words, the 100 per cent aggregates less all amounts allocated to the first Line and all three Surplus Treaties. Copy the formula across as far as column U and down as far as row 18. The results will look like this:

	S	T	U
7		Facultative	
8	Aggregates	Premiums	Losses
9	0	0	0
10	0	0	0
11	0	0	0
12	0	0	0
13	0	0	0
14	0	0	0
15	0	0	0
16	12	0	0
17	18,669,666	19,267	9,120
18	23,044,955	24,385	0
19	40,081,554	41,563	0

We now have a model which will allocate the aggregates, premiums and losses from a historical profile over the treaty programme of our choice.

However, we have not yet totalled any of the columns, or performed any other kind of analysis on the results. What we need is a way of estimating the net result to the Reinsured and to the hypothetical treaties.

As previously explained, we will regard the Reinsured's profit as retained premiums plus reinsurance commission less retained losses and excess of loss reinsurance costs. The last item is beyond the scope of this model, and so we shall ignore it for the time being. We also want to look at the hypothetical treaty results, being premiums less commissions and losses, as well as the balance of each treaty and the amount of aggregate to the retention and each treaty. The last aspect will have a bearing on the cost of catastrophe protection, and the attractiveness to Reinsurers of the offered treaties.

We need to calculate the maximum sum insured limit of the retention and each of the Quota Share, First, Second and Third Surplus treaties. These can go into cells B34 to B38, leaving the corresponding cells in column A for appropriate labels.

The formula for calculating the value in cell B34 is:

+B32*(100−E32)/100

In other words, the amount of the first Line of retention, times the difference between 100 and the percentage ceded to the Quota Share Treaty. We are dividing by 100 because we have expressed the percentage cession as a whole number, e.g. 70. If we had entered 0.7 and formatted the cell as a percentage, the formula would be +B32*(1−E32). This is a matter of personal preference.

In B35 we are calculating the sum insured limit of the Quota Share Treaty (the ceded amount). The formula is:

+B32*E32/100

The limits of the First, Second and Third Surplus Treaties, shown in cells B36, B37 and B38 are, respectively:

+B32*E32
+B32*I32
+B32*K32

The aggregates are totalled as follows:

Caption (Row A)	Cell Address	Formula
Retention	C34	@SUM(G9..G19)*(100−E32)/100
Quota Share	C35	@SUM(G9..G19)*E32/100
1st Surplus	C36	@SUM(J9..J19)
2nd Surplus	C37	@SUM(M9..M19)
3rd Surplus	C38	@SUM(P9..P19)

68 Designing a Property Reinsurance Programme

Next, the premiums:

Caption	Cell Address	Formula
Retention	D34	@SUM(H9..H19)*(100 − E32)/100
Quota Share	D35	@SUM(H9..H19)*E32/100
1st Surplus	D36	@SUM(K9..K19)
2nd Surplus	D37	@SUM(N9..N19)
3rd Surplus	D38	@SUM(Q9..Q19)
Facultative	D39	@SUM(T9..T19)

Similarly for the losses, we have

Caption	Cell Address	Formula
Retention	E34	@SUM(I9..I19)*(100 − E32)/100
Quota Share	E35	@SUM(I9..I19)*E32/100
1st Surplus	E36	@SUM(L9..L19)
2nd Surplus	E37	@SUM(O9..O19)
3rd Surplus	E38	@SUM(R9..R19)
Facultative	E39	@SUM(U9..U19)

We can then work out the loss ratio for the retention, all treaties and the facultative account. We shall calculate the loss ratio for the retention in cell F34 as:

@IF(@ISERR(E34/D34*100),0,E34/D34*100)

In simple terms, we could just say E34/D34*100 i.e. losses over premiums, expressed as a percentage. However, computers cannot divide by zero. Therefore, if the value in cell D34 were a zero, we would get an answer of ERR (short for Error). We therefore introduce a new function @ISERR which says that if the result of E34/D34 is ERR, put 0, otherwise, put the result. Copy this formula as far as F39.

Now we are going to put in some assumed rates of commission for each treaty, as well as the facultative placements. These may vary tremendously from country to country and depending upon the state of the reinsurance market. We shall put these values into cells G35 to G39 (note that there is no commission on the retained premiums).

	G	H
33	Commission %	Commission
34		
35	40	0

	G	H
36	35	84,543
37	32.5	13,363
38	30	10,628
39	27.5	23,434

We shall then work out the monetary commission amounts in cells H35 to H39 using the formula:

+ D35*G35/100

and copying down as far as H39 (see sample results above).

We can then work out the results of each treaty in cells I35 to I38. The result is simply the premium less commission and losses, and so cell I35 will contain the formula:

+ D35 − E3 − H35

and copied down as far as I38 (I39 is not a treaty).

Finally, we want to see the net profit to the Reinsured. This can go almost anywhere in the model, but I have put it in cell G41, leaving the cells to the left of it clear for the caption, which could be a verbal representation of the formula explained above. The formula is:

+ D34 + @SUM(H36..H39) − E34

If you build the model and enter our sample data, you will come to the conclusion that this is not a very attractive book of business. However, we are only looking at one section of the portfolio, one earthquake zone and one year's underwriting result.

Taking a Line of $250,000 and no Quota Share Treaty, four Lines of First Surplus, two Lines of Second Surplus and three Lines of Third Surplus, the Reinsured ends up retaining $240,516,109 of aggregates. The estimated profit is $194,528 based on assumed rates of commission of 35, 32.5, 30 and 27.5 per cent for the First Surplus through to Facultative placements.

If we were to increase the Line to $500,000 but with a 50 per cent Quota Share Treaty, paying 40 per cent commission, the profit would be $151,428 against retained aggregates of $166,470,829. We would then need to establish whether the loss of $43,000 profit would be offset by the savings in the cost of catastrophe excess of loss protection as a result of the retained aggregates reducing by about one third.

Clearly, if we were to take a retention of $500,000 without a Quota Share Treaty, our retained profit would be $302,856 against retained aggregates of $332,941,658. We would then need to estimate the cost of a per risk excess of loss protection for $250,000 as well as the cost of increased catastrophe cover in order to judge whether to risk such an increase in the retention.

We shall deal with excess of loss costs in a later chapter.

CHAPTER 6

EXCESS OF LOSS COVERS

We have already come across excess of loss reinsurance as a type of facultative cover. Facultative reinsurances protect individual risks, and so when we arrange a facultative excess of loss reinsurance we are protecting against individual losses whose amounts exceed a fixed threshold (known as the "deductible" or "priority").

Excess of loss treaties, on the other hand, protect a large number of risks of different sizes, and can be designed to perform different functions, such as:

- to protect the reinsured against large individual losses;
- to protect the reinsured against an accumulation of smaller losses from a single event;
- to protect the reinsured against an accumulation of losses over a certain period.

Sometimes an excess of loss programme will combine more than one of the above functions.

In many cases, excess of loss reinsurance is purchased alongside proportional reinsurance and protects the reinsured's retained account.

For example, a company may have a Quota Share Treaty with a limit of $1 million sum insured, any one risk and a retention of 25 per cent. Because the risks in the company's portfolio have differing sums insured, the company will not have a $250,000 retention on every single risk. For example, on a risk with a sum insured of $500,000 the company's maximum commitment will be $125,000. If the company arranges an excess of loss protection with a priority of $125,000 for any single risk, even a total loss on a $500,000 risk would not give rise to a loss under the cover.

Risk excess of loss treaties

Going back to the functions of excess of loss treaties, we can see that the company has a proportional treaty programme to provide it with underwriting capacity. The company has decided that the maximum amount it can pay in respect of any of its policies is $125,000. It could have taken a 12.5 per cent retention under the $1 million Quota Share Treaty, but has instead decided to take a 25 per cent retention and to protect its potential liability with a risk excess of loss treaty for $125,000 excess of $125,000.

The slip for such a protection might look like this:

Reinsured: XYZ Insurance Company

Period:: 12 months at 1 January 1996
Losses Occurring During Basis

Type: Excess of Loss Reinsurance

Interest: Protecting the Reinsured's retention of up to US$250,000 sum insured, any one risk, in respect of all business underwritten in the Reinsured's Fire Department, including Burglary when written in conjunction with Fire business.

Territorial Scope: Bermuda

Sum Reinsured: To pay up to US$125,000 Ultimate Net Loss each and every loss occurrence, any one risk
Excess of US$125,000 Ultimate Net Loss each and every loss occurrence, any one risk.

Conditions: Ultimate Net Loss Clause
Net Retained Lines Clause
Reinsured to be sole judge of what constitutes any one risk
Nuclear Energy Risks Exclusion Clause, NMA 1975a
Excluding obligatory and excess of loss reinsurances
War and Civil War Exclusion Clause

Reinstatement: Two full reinstatements at additional premium calculated at pro rata to amount reinstated, irrespective of time.

Premium: Minimum and Deposit Premium US$40,000 payable in four equal instalments on 1 January, 1 April, 1 July and 1 October 1996, adjustable at 5% of the Reinsured's Gross Net Premium Income accounted during the period of this agreement.

Information: Information presentation dated 15 November 1995 seen by reinsurers hereon.
Estimated GNPI: US$900,000

Note the way in which the cover limit and priority are worded "To pay up to US$125,000 Ultimate Net Loss each and every loss occurrence, any one risk, excess of...". It is this form of words which distinguishes a risk excess of loss cover from any other kind of cover. If the Reinsured's portfolio is affected by a catastrophic loss in which several of its insured risks are damaged or destroyed at the same time, this type of cover will only pay individual claims which have exceeded the priority. The Reinsured cannot add the claims together for the purpose of collecting from a risk excess of loss protection.

Excess of Loss Covers

Catastrophe Excess of Loss Treaties

These treaties, on the other hand, are designed to respond to just such a situation, by allowing the Reinsured to add together all his net retained losses from a single event, in order to make a single excess of loss claim. A catastrophe excess of loss slip might look like this:

Reinsured: XYZ Insurance Company

Period:: 12 months at 1 January 1996
Losses Occurring During Basis

Type: Excess of Loss Reinsurance

Interest: Protecting the Reinsured's retention of up to US$250,000 sum insured, any one risk, in respect of all business underwritten in the Reinsured's Fire Department, including Burglary when written in conjunction with Fire business

Territorial Scope: Bermuda

Sum Reinsured: To pay up to US$875,000 Ultimate Net Loss any one loss occurrence
Excess of US$125,000 Ultimate Net Loss any one loss occurrence

Conditions: Ultimate Net Loss Clause
Net Retained Lines Clause
Definition of "any one loss occurrence" as per LPO 98a
Two Risk Warranty
Nuclear Energy Risks Exclusion Clause, NMA 1975a
Excluding obligatory and excess of loss reinsurances
War and Civil War Exclusion Clause

Reinstatement: Two full reinstatements at additional premium calculated at pro rata to amount reinstated, irrespective of time

Premium: Minimum and Deposit Premium US$40,000 payable in four equal instalments on 1 January, 1 April, 1 July and 1 October 1996, adjustable at 5% of the Reinsured's Gross Net Premium Income accounted during the period of this agreement

Information: Information presentation dated 15 November 1995 seen by reinsurers hereon
Reinsured has in force a risk excess of loss cover for US$125,000 excess of US$125,000 with two reinstatements, which shall be deemed to be in force at the time of any occurrence giving rise to a loss hereunder
Estimated GNPI: US$900,000

Note the different wording of the contract limit, "To pay up to US$875,000 Ultimate Net Loss any one loss occurrence". In this case there is no need for the Reinsured to suffer individual losses of more than $125,000 per risk. The

74 Excess of Loss Covers

fact that a number of losses can be attributed to a single event means that the Reinsured can add together his net losses from the event, and recover any amount which exceeds the priority of his catastrophe reinsurance programme.

Note that in this example we have taken the same amount of $125,000 as the priority for each cover. Since a catastrophe cover is only designed to pay claims arising from a catastrophic situation (involving more than one insured risk in the same event), there should be some mechanism to ensure that the cover does not expose reinsurers to a loss on a single risk.

The example assumes that both the risk excess of loss and the catastrophe excess of loss covers are in existence at the same time. If there is a catastrophe occurrence, losses on individual risks exceeding $125,000 each will fall to the risk excess of loss programme first. The total retained losses from the occurrence, less recoveries, if any from the risk excess of loss cover will form the "Ultimate Net Loss" of the Reinsured for the purpose of making recoveries under the catastrophe (see Table 6).

Table 6: A simple example of risk and catastrophe excess of loss covers working in practice

Sum Insured	Retention %	Quota Share %	100% Loss	Retained Loss
2,000,000	12.5	37.5	1,000,000	125,000
1,000,000	25	75	1,000,000	250,000[1]
500,000	25	75	200,000	50,000
				425,000
				− 125,000
			U.N.L.	300,000
			Priority	− 125,000
			Recovery	175,000

[1] Results in a $125,000 recovery under the risk excess of loss cover.

As you can see in the example in Table 6, it would not be possible for the catastrophe cover to be exposed to a loss from a single risk, due to the existence of the risk excess of loss cover. In fact, the risk cover in our example provides two full reinstatements of the limit. This means that even if there were several losses above $125,000 from the same event, the Reinsured could make multiple recoveries from the risk excess cover, up to a total of $375,000.

Another mechanism which is frequently used in catastrophe covers is known as the "Two Risk Warranty" which states that the catastrophe reinsurers will only be liable to pay claims when two or more insured risks are affected in the same event.

As with all reinsurance matters, there are infinite possibilities. For example, if the same catastrophe cover existed without there being a risk cover alongside it, and without the two risk warranty, the cover would respond to both large individual losses and to catastrophe losses. The net losses of $425,000 would not be reduced by any risk excess of loss protection and $300,000 would be recoverable from the cover.

In these circumstances, the cover combines the functions of risk and catastrophe covers. The cost of such a cover would be greater than for a pure catastrophe cover, because it is now also exposed to losses on single risks.

While many excess of loss covers are designed to protect against abnormal occurrences, there are other covers which give protection against an abnormal number of smaller losses accumulating over the course of a year.

Working Excess of Loss Covers

These have a priority which is fixed at a low level. This means that the cover will almost certainly be affected by several losses every single year. The reinsured is protecting himself against an unusually large number of losses of this magnitude during the year. A good example of a working excess of loss cover is the first layer of a motor excess of loss programme. Because these covers anticipate a certain number of losses each year, reinsurers charge a premium which is sufficient to pay the anticipated losses, plus a further premium against the possibility of more, unforeseen losses. This is usually achieved by charging a variable rate, adjustable in accordance with the amount of losses to the cover, once known. This is called "Burning Cost Rating" and is discussed later in this book.

Stop Loss Covers

These are sometimes referred to as "Excess of Loss Ratio Covers", which is a far more descriptive term. They are most often used to protect a crop insurance account against weather perils, most commonly hailstorm, where it is often the only form of reinsurance cover available. A company which underwrites a crop hail account knows that hailstorms will strike somewhere every year, but has a good idea of how much the claims are going to be in relation to his overall premium (i.e. the loss ratio).

For example, the annual premium from crop insurance may be around $10 million and the average losses around $7.5 million giving an expected loss ratio of 75 per cent. Costs of administration and loss adjustment may be around 15 per cent of premiums, giving the company an annual profit of 10 per cent.

The company wants to protect itself against a bad year, which may only happen once every 20 years or so, and which could push his loss ratio up to 200 per cent.

The job of reinsurers is not to guarantee a profit to the Reinsured, but merely to reduce his risk of ruin. It would therefore not be possible to cover in excess of a loss ratio of 75 per cent. A more likely figure for the Reinsured's priority would be 100 per cent.

Let us assume that the cover is arranged to protect the Reinsured for any loss amount in excess of 100 per cent of the year's gross premium income, up to a further 100 per cent. The cover is assumed to cost 5 per cent of the gross premium income.

Taking the above figures, in a normal year the Reinsured would pay 75 per cent of the premiums as losses; 15 per cent would go on administration costs and 5 per cent on the reinsurance premium, leaving a 5 per cent profit margin.

If the loss ratio for the year was 200 per cent, the Reinsured would recover 100 per cent from the reinsurers. He would therefore have paid away 100 per cent in losses (net of reinsurance recoveries), 15 per cent in administration costs and 5 per cent as reinsurance premium, leaving his account in a deficit to the tune of 20 per cent of gross premiums.

A slip for such a cover may look like this:

Reinsured: XYZ Insurance Company

Period: 1996 harvesting season

Type: Stop Loss Reinsurance

Class: To cover the Reinsured's Crop Hail account

Sum Reinsured: To pay all losses excess of 100% of the Reinsured's Gross Net Premium Income or US$9,000,000 whichever is the greater, up to a further amount of 100% of the Reinsured's Gross Net Premium Income or US$11,000,000 whichever is the lesser

Premium: Minimum and Deposit Premium payable in full at inception, US$450,000 adjustable on expiry at 5% of the Reinsured's Gross Net Premium Income booked in respect of all crops with anticipated harvesting dates during 1996

Information: Information presentation dated 15 November 1995 seen by reinsurers hereon
Estimated Gross Net Premium Income US$10,000,000

As you can see in the specimen slip, the limit and the priority are expressed as percentages of the Gross Net Premium Income, as well as having monetary limits. The monetary figures are there to ensure that reinsurers will not be exposed too soon if the actual premium income is far less than expected. In our example the priority represents $10 million based upon the given estimate of the Gross Net Premium Income, but if the Reinsured has miscalculated, and only booked $1 million of premium, the reinsurers might then be exposed to losses from a single hailstorm, instead of simply being exposed in an unusually bad year. The existence of the $9 million minimum monetary priority will give the reinsurers some security against this, whilst giving the Reinsured a "hedge" against a drop of up to 10 per cent in his premium income.

Conversely, if the company managed to generate $20 million of income, the financial exposure of the reinsurers would be doubled without an upper monetary limit. The existence of the $11 million upper limit enables reinsurers to avoid this situation, whilst allowing the Reinsured a 10 per cent margin for growth.

FINANCIAL ASPECTS

An excess of loss contract is far simpler, in an accounting sense, than a proportional treaty, because there are usually only three types of financial transaction, namely premium, loss payments and reinstatement premiums.

Premium

A proportional treaty accepts percentage cessions of individual policies, and therefore receives the same percentages of the premiums for those policies. An excess of loss contract is different, because it protects the Reinsured against losses over a certain size.

We have already seen that for facultative excess of loss reinsurances the premium is disproportionate, because most losses are only partial. In fact, losses of 40 per cent or less of the full value at risk may amount to 80 per cent of the total of all losses.

The premium for an excess of loss contract is based upon the reinsurer's assessment of the risk he is assuming, and this will depend upon a number of factors, such as:

- the maximum amount being protected (i.e. the Reinsured's retained "line");
- the profile of the protected account (numbers of risks within bands of values);
- loss history;
- catastrophe exposure;
- original premium income;
- the limit and deductible of the cover.

Rate

The rating calculations which the reinsurer performs will enable him to fix a premium for the contract. This premium, expressed as a percentage of the contract limit, is known as the "Rate on Line", which is often used by reinsurers in their premium calculations. The Rate on Line is important to reinsurers, as it gives a quick indication of the payback period, should the contract suffer a total loss. For example, if a contract has a limit of $10 million and the annual contract premium is $2 million the reinsurers would need to collect $2 million per year for five years, in order to pay for a single loss of $10 million.

Having formed an opinion as to the amount of premium he requires to protect the Reinsured, the reinsurer will usually express the premium as a percentage rate, applied to some variable component of the business he is protecting. This variability is necessary in order to ensure that if the Reinsured's business grows, the reinsurer will receive more premium for the increased exposure under the reinsurance contract.

Premium income

The most common variable to which a rate may be applied is the protected premium income. Ignoring changes in the Reinsured's original premium rates, growth in the premium income usually indicates that more risks are being accepted, leading to an increase in reinsurers' exposure under the excess of loss contract.

The most frequently used term to describe the premium income is "Gross Net Premium Income", or "GNPI". A typical definition of GNPI may be found in the specimen wordings in Appendix 5, but essentially, "Gross" means the premiums booked by the Reinsured during the contract period, without any deduction for brokerages, taxes or other expenses. "Net" means net of the cost of any other reinsurances which have the effect of reducing the exposure to reinsurers under the excess of loss contract. In other words, we are rating the contract based upon the protected portion of the original gross premiums. Premiums paid for facultative and proportional treaty reinsurances may therefore be deducted from the gross booked premium in order to arrive at the GNPI. However, premiums paid for other excess of loss contracts should not be deducted. This is so that, if the reinsurer is rating an entire excess of loss programme, with several layers of cover, some of which may be per risk covers and others catastrophe, he will have a common income upon which to base his rates, rather than having to reduce the GNPI by the amount of premium he is charging for any underlying layers.

(Minimum and) Deposit Premium

Most excess of loss contracts have a variable premium which can only be accurately calculated after the contract has expired. It is therefore usual for reinsurers to charge a Deposit Premium at the beginning of the period, and to adjust it when the variable factors are known.

Sometimes, one or more of these variables can be unexpectedly low, resulting in an unacceptably low contract premium, after application of the rate. Reinsurers are effectively selling their capacity to different Reinsureds throughout the year, and their own capacity is limited by the size of their capital and their own reinsurance protections (retrocessions). Reinsurers therefore require a Minimum Premium for any contract which they accept, so that, even if the final GNPI is negligible, they will still receive sufficient premium to cover their own costs and exposure.

Usually, the Minimum Premium and the Deposit Premium are the same figure, but there are some instances where two different figures are specified. When the two figures are the same, we refer to a "Minimum and Deposit Premium" or "M & D". Hence, we may see a contract premium described in the following way:

"Minimum and Deposit Premium US$4,500,000 payable in four equal quarterly instalments on 1st January, 1st April, 1st July and 1st October, 1996, adjustable upon expiry at 10% of the Reinsured's Gross Net Premium Income accounted during the period of this agreement."

Deposit premiums are frequently paid annually, half yearly or quarterly, and usually in advance. Reinsurers will often discount the Deposit Premium according to the speed with which he collects it. For example, if the Deposit Premium is to be paid in full at inception, there may be a 20 per cent discount from the estimated final contract premium. If the premium is to be paid half-yearly, the discount may only be 10 per cent, whilst if the premium is payable in quarterly instalments, there may be little or no discount. This discount is only from the "up front" premium. The finally adjusted premium will be the same, unless of course, the adjusted figure is much lower than expected. In such circumstances, assuming that the Deposit Premium was the same as the Minimum Premium, an 80 per cent M & D will result in a lower final contract premium than one with the same rate, but with a 100 per cent M & D.

The "penal" M & D

If in our above example, the final GNPI is $40 million the 10 per cent rate would produce an adjusted premium of $4 million. However, the Minimum and Deposit Premium was $4.5 million and there will therefore be a nil premium adjustment. In such cases, the M & D is said to be penal, because the Reinsured is effectively being punished for incorrectly estimating his premium. This often happens with new insurance companies which make optimistic projections for the purpose of putting together a business plan.

Worked example

The contract limit is $10 million any one loss occurrence.
The estimated GNPI is $50 million.
The required Rate on Line is 50 per cent producing a contract premium of $5 million which represents 10 per cent of the estimated GNPI.
The Reinsured might charge a Minimum and Deposit Premium of $4.5 million at the beginning of the year (the inception of the contract), and adjust this at the end of the year, based upon 10 per cent of the actual GNPI.

If, at the end of the period, the actual GNPI has risen to $60 million it usually means that the Reinsured has accepted more business than he had originally estimated. The 10 per cent adjustment rate, applied to the actual

80 Excess of Loss Covers

GNPI produces a contract premium of $6 million (or a 60 per cent Rate on Line), meaning that the Reinsured must pay an adjustment premium of $1.5 million to the reinsurers, in order to "top up" the Deposit Premium to the actual earned premium.

Other variable factors

Although GNPI is the most common variable used to adjust an excess of loss contract premium, it is by no means the only one. For example, a Personal Accident protection on a pension fund might be rated at five cents per member, based upon the average membership measured at 12-monthly intervals. Cash in Transit covers may be rated based on annual carryings, and Employers' Liability covers on North Sea oil rigs may be rated on the number of man days spent offshore. There is no limit to the variety of factors which may be used as a basis for rating excess of loss covers.

Another variable which is commonly used in the rating of working excess of loss covers is the amount of losses which the reinsurers sustain under the contract. This form of rating, which is retrospective in nature, is referred to as "Burning Cost" and is described later.

Loss payments

Loss payments are simple transactions, once the Ultimate Net Loss has been established. However, establishing the Ultimate Net Loss is not always simple. Indeed, it is sometimes difficult even to know how many losses there have been, and when the losses have taken place. There are many factors which can influence the claim collection. The following are useful examples:

"Hours Clause"

Although commonly referred to as the Hours Clause, this is actually a definition of the duration and extent of a catastrophe, which is found within a clause called "Definition of Any One Loss Occurrence" which has a wording similar to the following:

"For the purposes of this Agreement a loss occurrence shall consist of all individual insured losses which are the direct and immediate result of the sudden violent physical operation of one and the same manifestation of an original insured peril and occur during a loss period of 72 hours any:

(a) hurricane, typhoon, windstorm, rainstorm, hailstorm or tornado;
(b) earthquake, seaquake, tidal wave or volcanic eruption;
(c) fire;
(d) riot or civil commotion which occurs within the limits of one city, town or village; or
(e) 168 consecutive hours as regards all other insured perils.

It is further agreed that all individual insured losses which are the direct and immediate result of:

(i) malicious damage which occurs within the limits of one City, Town or Village during a loss period of 72 consecutive hours shall constitute an individual loss occurrence for the purposes of this Agreement; as shall

(ii) any flood or floods which occur within the catchment area of any named river and its tributaries during a loss period of 168 consecutive hours. It being understood that for the purposes of this Article a flood shall mean the escape of water from its normal confines (other than tanks, apparatus, pipes and similar water containers forming part of buildings).

Provided that if any such aforementioned operation and physical manifestation shall directly and immediately result in the physical manifestation of another original insured peril or perils then all individual insured losses which directly and immediately result therefrom and occur during the same loss period of 168 consecutive hours or 72 consecutive hours where any of the perils mentioned in (a) (b) (c) and (d) above are involved shall be deemed to constitute a single loss occurrence.

The Reinsured may choose the date and time when the appropriate loss period commences provided that no such period shall commence earlier than the time of the first recorded individual insured loss to which this Agreement applied resulting from the operation and manifestation of an original insured peril as aforesaid and if the operation of such a peril shall last longer than the appropriate loss period then the Reinsured may apply further appropriate loss periods in respect of the continued operation of that period provided none of those additional periods shall overlap."

In other words, if the Reinsured suffers a series of losses as a result of freezing winter weather conditions (a 168 hour event for the purposes of the clause) lasting 16 days, the Reinsured may divide the period into several individual loss occurrences in order to recover from his catastrophe cover. Since 168 hours equals seven days, there appears to be a possibility of dividing the loss occurrence into three separate loss occurrences.

The question is, how can this be done in a way which is most advantageous to the Reinsured?

We should bear in mind that for each separate loss occurrence, the Reinsured will have to bear one deductible under his catastrophe programme. We should also look at the number of reinstatements available under the catastrophe programme, as well as the adequacy of the cover limit.

PRACTICAL EXERCISE 3: ALLOCATING CLAIMS OVER AN EXCESS OF LOSS PROGRAMME

In this exercise, we are going to look at the possible ways of allocating a loss of several days' duration over an excess of loss programme.

The company suffers a large number of individual losses from a winter freeze. The renewal of the company's excess of loss arrangements takes place on 1 January, whilst the catastrophe is still in progress. The covers contain an Extended Expiration Clause, which states that should the covers expire whilst a covered loss event is in progress, the entire loss event is recoverable, provided that no portion of the claim from that event is claimed against next year's cover.

82 Excess of Loss Covers

The catastrophe covers contain a definition of each and every loss, which states that all freeze losses occurring within a period of 168 consecutive hours shall be regarded as one loss occurrence for the purposes of making recoveries from the catastrophe cover. The company may choose when to start each period of 168 hours (7 days), provided no period starts before the time of the first recorded loss to the company, and provided no two periods overlap.

The company should therefore decide how to divide the period into separate seven-day periods, in order to gain the maximum recovery, net of reinstatement premiums, from its reinsurance programme.

Please bear in mind that recoveries from the risk excess of loss programme must be deducted first.

The amounts of each loss, *net of proportional reinsurance recoveries* are as follows:

Date of loss	Loss to net retention
28/12/94	20,000
29/12/94	50,000
30/12/94	70,000
31/12/94	100,000
01/01/95	0
02/01/95	210,000
02/01/95	400,000
03/01/95	80,000
04/01/95	300,000
04/01/95	200,000
06/01/95	50,000
07/01/95	100,000
08/01/95	70,000
09/01/95	70,000
10/01/95	400,000
11/01/95	120,000
12/01/95	50,000

The company had the following excess of loss programmes:

1994:

Per Risk:
$750,000 XS $250,000 each and every loss, each and every risk
Premium: $100,000
Reinstatements: 2 at 100% additional premium

Catastrophe:
1st Layer:
$650,000 XS $350,000 any one loss occurrence
Premium $40,000
Reinstatements: 1 at 100%

2nd Layer:
$1,000,000 XS $1,000,000 any one loss occurrence
Premium $50,000
Reinstatements: 1 at 100%

1995:

Per Risk:
$750,000 XS $250,000 each and every loss, each and every risk
Premium: $120,000
Reinstatements: 2 at 100%

Catastrophe:
1st Layer:
$650,000 XS $350,000 any one loss occurrence
Premium $44,000
Reinstatements: 1 at 100%
2nd Layer:
$1,000,000 XS $1,000,000 any one loss occurrence
Premium $55,000
Reinstatements: 1 at 100%

All covers commence on 1 January
All covers have an Extended Expiration Clause
The catastrophe covers have a limitation per loss occurrence, as follows:

> 72 hours for Wind, Flood and Earthquake;
> 168 hours for losses from any other cause.

- Calculate the loss recoveries from the per-risk covers, as well as the reinstatement premiums.
- Calculate the most advantageous way of recovering under the catastrophe programme, bearing in mind the provisions of the "Hours Clause".

(See Appendix 3 for answers to Practical Exercise 3.)

Reinstatement Premiums

Most excess of loss contracts are designed to pay losses above a certain size, per loss occurrence, and have a fixed maximum amount which the reinsurers can pay for a single event.

Some contracts do not place any limitation upon the numbers of events which the reinsurers may be liable for in all. Consequently, reinsurers under such contracts have potentially unlimited liability. Such contracts are becoming increasingly rare, as reinsurers attempt to limit their liability, but are still seen in some areas, particularly in motor insurance.

More commonly, reinsurers limit the maximum amount which the reinsurance contract can pay, in the aggregate for the contract period. A common way of achieving this is to state that the contract limit applies only once during the contract period, and that any losses which the reinsurers pay will erode that limit. For example, if the contract limit is $10 million any one loss occurrence, excess of $5 million any one loss occurrence, a $7.5 million loss would result in a $2.5 million loss to the cover. This would erode the cover limit, leaving $7.5 million available to cover future losses.

Note, however, that future losses would still be subject to the contract deductible of $5 million.

Often, the Reinsured will not feel comfortable with a single limit of liability, and will wish to reinstate the contract limit to its full amount after each loss, so that he will always have the benefit of full cover.

Such reinstatements, which are usually limited in number, are subject to the payment of an additional premium to the reinsurers. This is known as the "Reinstatement Premium" and is usually payable at the same time as the loss is paid by the reinsurers. The standard practice is that the reinstatement premium is deducted from the claim payment.

Reinstatement premiums are calculated as a percentage of the basic contract premium, and if a reinstatement premium becomes payable before the contract premium has been adjusted, it will be provisionally calculated based upon the Deposit Premium.

The following reinstatement conditions are common:

- *At nil additional premium*: The contract limit will be automatically reinstated from the time of the loss occurrence, free of charge.
- *At 100% additional premium*: The contract limit will be automatically reinstated from the time of the loss occurrence, at an additional premium calculated at pro-rata as to the amount reinstated, irrespective of time. This means that if the loss is 50 per cent of the contract limit, the additional premium to reinstate the limit will be 50 per cent of the contract premium. Similarly, if the percentage additional premium is specified as 50 per cent a loss of 50 per cent of the contract limit would require the payment of 25 per cent (50 per cent of 50 per cent) of the basic premium in order to reinstate the contract limit to its full amount.
- *At pro-rata to time and amount*: A loss of 50 per cent of the contract limit, which occurs 10 days before the expiry of a 12-month contract period, would require a reinstatement premium calculated at 50 per cent of 10/365ths of the contract premium.

Reinsurers are becoming increasingly reluctant to grant reinstatement premiums with a pro-rata to time factor. Their argument is that they are providing cover against losses which may occur at any time during the year. The reinstatement premium is a part of their payback calculations, so that a contract with a 25 per cent Rate on Line with a single reinstatement at 100 per cent additional premium can suffer a maximum loss in a year of twice the contract limit. In the event of a single total loss, 100 per cent of the contract limit would become payable, so that, in effect, the reinsurer has only lost the equivalent of 50 per cent of the contract limit (i.e. the contract limit, less two premiums, each equivalent to 25 per cent of the limit). Of course, if there is a second total loss, no further reinstatement premium is payable, leaving the reinsurers out of pocket to the tune of 150 per cent of the contract limit. If the reinstatement premium were to be reduced pro-rata to the number of days' cover remaining, the additional premium would be anything from 100 per cent if the loss occurred on the first day of the cover, to virtually nothing, if the loss occurred on the last day of the cover.

Note that if reinstatements are stated in the contract, the limit must be reinstated following a loss. The Reinsured cannot choose not to reinstate the contract, if for example, he suffers a loss on the last day of the contract period.

Contracts with a high loss expectancy (and consequently a high Rate on Line) can give some surprising results when reinstatement premiums are considered. For example, a contract with a 60 per cent Rate on Line and a $10 million limit per occurrence with one reinstatement at 100 per cent will produce the following results:

- *If there is no loss*: $6 million profit to the reinsurers (less brokerage).
- *If there is a loss of $5 million to the contract*: $4 million profit to the reinsurers (Basic premium of $6 million plus $3 million to reinstate 50 per cent of the limit, less $5 million loss).
- *If there is a $10 million loss to the contract*: $2 million profit to the reinsurers (Premium of $6 million plus $6 million to reinstate 100 per cent of the limit, less $10 million loss).
- *If there are two $10 million losses to the contract*: $8 million loss to the reinsurers (Premium $6 million plus reinstatement premium of $6 million less two losses of $10 million).

Sometimes there may be a number of reinstatements of the contract limit, at different levels of reinstatement premium, e.g., One free, plus one at 50 per cent plus two at 100 per cent. These must be taken in sequence, so that if the contract limit is $10 million, reinstatement of the first $10 million of losses to the contract will be free, reinstatement of the next $10 million of losses will be based on 50 per cent of the contract premium, and reinstatement of the next $20 million of losses will be based upon 100 per cent of the contract premium.

BURNING COST RATING

It has been customary for many years to rate working excess of loss covers on a burning cost basis. What is the reasoning behind this method of rating?

86 Excess of Loss Covers

Working covers

The term "working cover" is applied to a low layer excess of loss contract which regularly suffers losses. The best example is a motor excess of loss cover where the reinsured's priority is low enough to ensure that the layer will be affected by a significant number of losses each year (e.g. less than the value of an average vehicle or a fairly typical damages award for bodily injury or minor third party property damage).

Assuming that the protected portfolio is quite large and homogeneous, the frequency of smaller losses can be estimated quite reliably and a working layer will therefore be rated on the basis that a certain level of losses can be reasonably anticipated each year.

This results in reinsurers charging a premium to cover the anticipated claims (as well as their own administration costs), plus a further amount to cover the risk of incurring more than the anticipated amount of claims.

Definition of Burning Cost

"Burning Cost" means the rate of premium which must be charged in order to match the incurred losses to the layer.

For example, if the reinsured's retained premium income is $10 million and the incurred losses to its working cover are $1 million the contract rate would need to be 10 per cent of retained premium income in order for the reinsurers to "break even". In this example, the 10 per cent rate is known as the "Pure Burning Cost".

Actually, reinsurers would argue that charging a rate of 10 per cent in the above example would leave them in a deficit situation because they have to pay brokerage (in some cases) as well as their own administrative costs. To compensate for this, reinsurers will load the Pure Burning Cost by a factor of 100/70, 100/75 or 100/80 to produce a "Loaded Burning Cost".

The most common loading factor is probably 100/70ths and it allows reinsurers a margin of nearly 43 per cent of the incurred losses.

Burning Cost calculations are performed retrospectively, when the incurred losses to the contract are known or can be estimated. This involves charging a deposit premium at the inception of the cover and adjusting it at the end of the year when the cover has expired.

Insurance claims, particularly those involving any kind of third party liability, can take several years to settle, and it is therefore usual to recalculate the excess of loss premium every year, until all of the claims have been settled.

The following example demonstrates how the process evolves.

The reinsured requires excess of loss protection for his motor account. From the historical claims information, the protection is broken down into several layers, and the working layer is established at $700,000 excess of $300,000 each and every claim.

The estimated retained premium income for the coming year is $41 million and the reinsurers anticipate that the layer will produce losses totalling between $500,000 and $1 million during the year. The Pure Burning Cost is therefore estimated at between 1.22 per cent and 2.44 per cent of the estimated retained premium income.

The reinsurers decide to rate the cover on a Burning Cost basis with a loading factor of 100/75ths.

A *minimum rate* of 0.65 per cent is charged. This is a fairly arbitrary figure which the leading reinsurer considers to be the minimum amount of premium he requires for the granting of reinsurance capacity. It is a means of guaranteeing that reinsurers will still receive a premium in the unlikely event that no losses affect the cover.

A *maximum rate* of 3.50 per cent is applied. This ensures that, if the eventual claims to the cover are significantly higher than anticipated, the Reinsured will begin to benefit from the cover, instead of paying ever-increasing premiums of 100/75ths of the claims he is recovering.

A *Minimum and Deposit Premium* is charged at the beginning of the year, or in instalments at regular intervals. This guarantees that the reinsurers will receive a minimum level of premium, even if the eventual retained premium income is considerably less than the original estimate. The Minimum and Deposit Premium is usually calculated by applying the minimum rate to the estimated retained premium income.

The premium of the working layer may therefore be expressed as follows:

"Minimum and Deposit Premium $266,500 payable in four equal quarterly instalments, adjustable at 100/75ths of the incurred losses hereon, subject to a minimum rate of 0.65% and a maximum rate of 3.50% of the Reinsured's *Gross Net Premium Income* for the period of this cover."

"Gross Net Premium Income" (GNPI) is the standard way of expressing gross retained premium income, and means the total premiums accepted by the reinsured during the period of the cover, without deducting anything for commission or brokerage paid away (i.e. gross), less premiums paid away for other reinsurances which have the effect of reducing claims to the excess of loss programme (reinsurances which inure to the benefit of the programme).

During the first year the reinsured pays the four instalments of the Minimum and Deposit Premium. A number of claims occur during the year, but not all of them are settled quickly. In fact, during the first year there are only three claims payments made by reinsurers, for amounts of $10,000, $11,125 and $25,000.

At the end of the first year the Reinsured declares his actual GNPI as $41,856,750. Paid losses, as we have just seen, total $46,125 and outstanding losses are declared at $550,000 to the working cover.

The premium adjustment is therefore as follows:

Incurred Losses = 46,125 + 550,000 = 596,125
GNPI = 41,856,750

Pure Burning Cost Rate = 1.424% (being 596,125 as a percentage of 41,856,750)
Loaded = 1.424 × 100/75 = 1.899%

88 Excess of Loss Covers

Reinsurance Premium = 41,856,750 × 1.899% = 794,860
Less Deposit Paid   266,500
Adjustment Premium payable   528,360

Over the next 12 months, some of the other claims are settled. Let us say that a total of $75,000 is paid by the reinsurers. Some of the claims which are settled by the Reinsured are much lower than originally reserved, and we end the second year with $250,000 of outstanding losses. The incurred loss position is now:

$46,125 + $75,000 + $250,000 = $371,125.

At this point, a second premium adjustment statement is prepared, as follows:

Pure Burning Cost Rate = 371,125/41,856,750 × 100/1 = 0.887%
Loaded rate = 0.887 × 100/75 = 1.182%

Reinsurance Premium = 41,856,750 × 1.182% = 494,747
Premium already paid   794,860
Refund due to reinsured   300,113

During the third year, a further $200,000 of claims are paid by the reinsurers and there are no outstanding losses at the end of the year. The incurred loss position is now:

$46,125 + $75,000 + $200,000 = $321,125.

At this point, a third and final premium adjustment statement is prepared, as follows:

Pure Burning Cost Rate = 321,125/41,856,750 × 100/1 = 0.767%
Loaded rate = 0.767 × 100/75 = 1.022%

Reinsurance Premium = 41,856,750 × 1.022% = 427,776
Premium already paid   494,747
Refund due to reinsured   66,971

In terms of cash flow, the Reinsured has gained nothing from the cover. In fact any claims recoveries he has made from his reinsurers are completely illusory, as he has paid his reinsurers $100 premium for every $75 of claims recoveries. What is worse, because at the end of the first year the outstanding losses were relatively high, a very large adjustment premium has been paid, giving reinsurers the benefit of a positive cash flow in anticipation of claims which did not materialise.

Clearly, a reinsurance contract only benefits the Reinsured when the claims exceed the contract premium. Often the reinsurance contract produces a profit for the reinsurers, or conversely, an expense for the Reinsured. This is essential in order to provide reinsurers with a fund which can be used to pay losses in "bad" years, as well as to provide reinsurers with an incentive to be in the business.

If a reinsurance contract is designed so that claims are likely to arise under it on a regular basis, it stands to reason that reinsurers will want to build these anticipated claims into their rating calculations, so that they will still be making a profit in normal years.

As we have seen, the Burning Cost method is a way of achieving this, but it has its drawbacks in terms of an unattractive cash flow from the Reinsured's point of view.

If the Reinsured only benefits from the excess of loss cover when the claims exceed the premiums, it seems strange to have a situation in which the contract premium is a variable figure which increases with each claim. In fact, the contract only begins to benefit the Reinsured after enough claims have occurred to push the Burning Cost above the maximum contract rate.

Often reinsurers have the benefit of historical claims figures and other information to enable them to estimate the likely amount of claims to the contract. They will use this information to pitch the maximum rate at such a level that they will only lose money in a very unusual year.

Therefore the question we should ask ourselves is, why have the contract at all?

There are some circumstances in which a working cover may be a fairly sensible option. For example, a new insurance company is usually capable of taking only a small retention. In an excess of loss contract this means the maximum amount which the Reinsured can pay in respect of each claim, before calling upon his reinsurers. This amount is generally known as the Reinsured's "priority" or "deductible".

Because the company is new, it has not built up any reserves from retained profits, and so it must initially set its priority at a low level. The reinsurers know from other similar business that there are likely to be regular losses exceeding this priority, but have no real way of knowing the size of the Reinsured's portfolio (e.g. the number of insured motor vehicles) and hence the likely number of claims. In these circumstances, reinsurers will feel safer with a Burning Cost rating formula.

The Reinsured may also feel happy to accept such a contract, because the minimum rate is likely to be quite low, which is important in terms of cash flow in the early years, where reinsurance costs are likely to represent a large proportion of the company's outgoings.

Nevertheless, as soon as a reasonably reliable pattern of loss experience is established, the Reinsured should try to move to a fixed rate by eliminating the "normal" losses from the reinsurance contract.

This may be done by increasing the priority to a level above the normal maximum loss amount. However, this solution may be unsatisfactory, because the Reinsured could suffer a large number of smaller losses in a single year. For example, unusually bad weather conditions could lead to a large number of road accidents. If the reinsurance priority is set at a high level, none of these claims might affect the contract, but the large numbers of claims could cause a severe strain upon the company's resources in the absence of any reinsurance recoveries.

An alternative method of eliminating the pointless cash swapping exercise would be to say, "For this layer of reinsurance protection, I am reasonably sure that I would claim an average of $750,000 per year from my reinsurers. I will therefore choose to pay the first $750,000 of reinsurance claims under this layer myself." In this way, reinsurers can concentrate upon charging a pure risk premium which is calculated to enable them to build up a reserve against a bad year (i.e. when claims to the layer go above $750,000). As there are no anticipated "normal" claims for the reinsurers to worry about, the reinsurers do not need to charge a floating rate.

This additional retention is known as an "Inner Aggregate Deductible" and in the following example it is compared to a similar contract rated on a Burning Cost basis.

BURNING COST SPREADSHEET MODEL

The best way to describe how a Burning Cost rated contract operates is by way of a spreadsheet model. We are going to build a simple spreadsheet to help us to look at the financial consequences of a contract which is rated on this basis. All we are really looking at is the difference between the amount of losses which the Reinsured can recover, and the premium he must pay for the contract. We are then going to compare this with the financial consequences of arranging the same cover, but with an Inner Aggregate Deductible and a fixed premium rate.

The first step is to put in some basic information. The GNPI is the Premium Income base which the contract is to be rated on. The heading goes into cell A4 and the figure into B4.

The Factor is the Burning Cost loading which appears in cell B5. The figure typed into the cell is 100/70 but because the cell is formatted to two decimal places, the result has been calculated as shown. The minimum and maximum rates are shown in cells B6 and B7, whilst the Minimum and Deposit Premium for the contract is in B8. The "To Earn" figures in C6 and C7 are just there for information, and show what the contract would earn at the minimum and maximum rates, based on the estimated GNPI.

	A	B	C
4	GNPI	750,000	
5	Factor	142,86%	To Earn:
6	Min Rate	1.00%	7,500
7	Max Rate	4.50%	33,750
8	MinDep	7,500	

Next, put some hypothetical loss figures in cells A11 to A21 or as far as you want to go. Note that these are losses to the layer, after the Reinsured's priority has been deducted from each claim.

The Premium column requires some calculation. The first cell to receive the formula is B11, and the formula reads as follows:

@IF(A11*$B$5<$B$8,$B$8,@IF(A11*$B$5>$B$4*$B$7,$B$4*$B$7,A11*$B$5))

This means that if the losses times the factor are less than the Minimum and Deposit Premium, put the Minimum and Deposit Premium. Failing that, if the losses times the factor are greater than the maximum rate applied to the GNPI, put the maximum rate applied to the GNPI. If both of these tests fail, then the losses multiplied by the factor must produce a premium which is somewhere between the minimum and the maximum rate applied to the GNPI, so calculate that. This formula can be copied into cells B12 downwards, as far as you like. Note that any reference to the figures for GNPI, factor, minimum rate or Minimum and Deposit Premium contain dollar signs around the cell address, so that they keep the same address whenever the formula is copied into another cell.

Column C contains a simple formula to calculate the balance of the contract, taking the contract losses payable by reinsurers away from the premium payable by the Reinsured. In cell C11 we simply need: +B11−A11 and copy the formula down.

	A	B	C
10	Losses to Layer	Premium	Balance
11	0	7,500	7,500
12	7,500	10,714	3,214
13	8,000	11,429	3,429
14	9,000	12,857	3,857
15	10,000	14,286	4,286
16	15,000	21,429	6,429
17	20,000	28,571	8,571
18	25,000	33,750	8,750
19	30,000	33,750	3,750
20	35,000	33,750	(1,250)
21	40,000	33,750	(6,250)

Now we are going to try an alternative basis of rating, using an Inner Aggregate Deductible and a fixed premium rate. "IAD" stands for "Inner Aggregate Deductible". The heading is in cell E6 and the figure itself is in F6. The figure for the rate is in F7 and is formatted to two places of decimals. This means that if you type in 0.0075 you will see 0.75%. The Minimum and Deposit Premium figure appears in cell F8. Finally, in G8 we have an earned premium figure, in order to calculate the premium should the rate applied to the GNPI produce less than the Minimum and Deposit Premium. The formula for this cell is:

@IF(B4*F7<F8,F8,B4*F7)

In other words, if the rate times the GNPI is less than the M & D, put the M & D, otherwise, multiply the GNPI by the Rate.

	E	F	G
4		Alternative Basis	
5			
6	IAD	28,125	
7	Rate	0.75%	To Earn:
8	MinDep	5,000	5,625

In cell E11 we calculate the recoverable losses to the contract, net of the Inner Aggregate Deductible. We use the formula:

@IF(A11<$F$6,0,A11−$F$6)

In other words, if the amount of losses otherwise recoverable under the contract is less than the Inner Aggregate Deductible, the contract pays nothing. If it is greater, the contract pays the losses otherwise recoverable, minus the Inner Aggregate Deductible.

The balance figures, from cell F11 downwards, represent the premium (cell G8) less the losses recoverable after deduction of the IAD, according to the formula:

$G$8−E11

Finally, the column headed "Advantage" represents the difference in balance between the Burning Cost basis and the IAD basis, i.e. C11−F11 and so on.

	E	F	G
10	Recoverable	Balance	Advantage
11	0	5,625	1,875[1]
12	0	5,625	(2,411)
13	0	5,625	(2,196)
14	0	5,625	(1,768)
15	0	5,625	(1,339)

	E	F	G
16	0	5,625	804
17	0	5,625	2,946
18	0	5,625	3,125
19	1,875	3,750	0
20	6,875	(1,250)	0
21	11,875	(6,250)	0

[1] Formula: C11 − F11

Having built the spreadsheet, you can play around with the figures to find an acceptable alternative to the Burning Cost. A very useful tool is the backsolver. For example, you may wish to convince the reinsurers that they would be no worse off on this new basis when the losses are very high. In order to keep the reinsurers' deficit the same on either basis at a particular level of losses, you can instruct the backsolver to make cell G21 equal zero, by changing the IAD (cell F6). This is how the figure of 28,125 was in fact arrived at.

If you change the IAD to $20,000 you can use the backsolver to make cell G20 equal 0 by changing the rate (cell F7). This produces a rate of 1.83 per cent which would be very unattractive to the Reinsured, because, not only would he be paying a higher premium at the beginning of the year, he would not make any loss recoveries in respect of the first 20,000 of incurred losses to the layer.

It is clear that some judgement must be used when using this model, because not every solution will be attractive. However, it is a useful tool, upon which you can perhaps improve to suit your own needs.

CHAPTER 7

EXCESS OF LOSS RATING

The rating of excess of loss contracts is a mixture of statistical theory, experience and intuition, tempered by the effects of market forces. Burning Cost rating is the easiest method to understand, because it simply involves determining the average annual incurred losses to the layer, loading it by an expense factor, and applying the resultant "premium" to the GNPI to produce a rate. Of course, there are some important factors to take into account, such as the effects of inflation upon the claims amounts, as well as the amount of the "usual" claims in relation to the size of the layer. For instance, if the individual claims to a contract, in excess of $200,000 are usually no more than $800,000 then that should be the contract limit. If no claims have ever exceeded that figure, then in theory, a Burning Cost calculation for a layer of $800,000 excess of $200,000 would produce the same rate as a layer of $1.8 million excess of $200,000. Clearly, the cover is being rated based upon the $800,000 limit. The next $1 million of cover should be separately rated.

EXPOSURE RATING

As we have already seen, an excess of loss cover on a single facultative risk may be rated as a percentage of the original policy premium using first loss rating scales. If you are unfamiliar with this method of rating, please refer to the section on facultative excess of loss on page 9 before proceeding.

It stands to reason that if we were protecting a group of risks on an excess of loss basis, we could apply the first loss scale to every protected risk, in order to arrive at a reasonable premium for an excess of loss cover. However, there are certain problems to overcome, such as the following.

1. Reinstatements

As we have seen, excess of loss contracts, particularly property covers, are subject to limited reinstatement of the contract limit following a loss. Usually, reinstatements are subject to the payment of an additional premium.

If we were protecting 100 individual risks by way of facultative reinsurance, each risk could result in a total loss to the reinsurers, and there would be no reinstatement premium to be paid, because any risk, once totally destroyed, would not expose the reinsurers any further.

Therefore, if we group these 100 risks together and protect them by a single excess of loss cover, with limited, paid reinstatements, we are restricting the extent of reinsurers' potential liability considerably. This should result in a premium discount, compared with the price for protecting the same 100 risks individually.

2. Differing values

It is highly unlikely that these 100 risks will all have the same insured value. In fact, in a typical "profile" of risks, there may be many whose values are below the proposed deductible of the excess of loss cover.

Let us assume that the Reinsured retains a maximum of $10 million per risk, and wishes to arrange an excess of loss programme in layers of $4 million excess of $1 million and $5 million excess of $5 million each loss, each risk.

- Risks with a Sum Insured of less than $1 million would not expose the programme at all.
- Risks with a Sum Insured of $2 million would expose only the first layer. They would effectively be protected for $1 million excess of $1 million or 50 per cent excess of 50 per cent of their insured value.
- Risks with a Sum Insured of $8 million would expose the first layer totally. The first layer coverage of $4 million excess of $1 million represents 50 per cent excess of 12.5 per cent of original insured values. The second layer would be exposed for $3 million excess of $5 million or 37.5 per cent excess of 62.5 per cent of original insured values.

Whilst there is no 100 per cent scientifically correct way of working out excess of loss costs, the following method can be used as a rough guide as to the sort of prices you might be expected to pay for a property, per-risk excess of loss programme.

1. The risk profile

This should be prepared for the protected portion of the account. In other words, if the Reinsured is protecting his net retention, then the risk profile should be in respect of net retention only. The profile should be prepared in "bands" of retained Sum Insured and should show the numbers of risks, the aggregate of retained Sums Insured and the aggregate of retained premiums (gross) for all risks within each band. Note that this profile is more detailed than the sort of profiles required for structuring a proportional treaty programme. In a proportional programme, we are concerned with the cession of risks, which, as we have seen, is usually done on a "top location and pro-rata" basis. We can therefore place each policy in the band corresponding to the Sum Insured of the highest valued risk in the policy schedule. When we are looking at a per-risk excess of loss programme, we are concerned with how each individual risk exposes the cover. If the profile were prepared with all of the premium for each policy being shown in the band corresponding to the value of the biggest risk, the profile would give a pessimistic picture of the true level of reinsurers' exposure.

In our risk profile we are going to assume that all of the risks in any given band have a Sum Insured exactly at the mid-point of the band. In other words, if the first band is from $0 to $1 million we shall assume that all of the risks within that band are valued at $500,000.

2. First Loss Scale

There are many First Loss Scales in existence, prepared by different insurance and reinsurance companies from their own statistical observations. Some companies prepare different scales for different types of business, such as commercial and industrial risks. We shall use the abbreviated scale given in Table 1 (see page 10).

Let us assume that we are rating a programme in layers of $4 million excess of $1 million and $5 million excess of $5 million. Risks in the band of values from $5 million to $6 million are taken to have an average value of $5.5 million. The $1 million priority will therefore represent 1/5.5 or the first 18 per cent of the average value. The first layer will be exposed to the next $4 million of risk. The priority plus the limit equals $5 million which is 5/5.5 or the first 91 per cent of the risk. If we round these figures to the nearest 10 per cent for simplicity's sake, we can say that the cover plus priority of the first layer represents 90 per cent of the insured values in this band of the risk profile. The priority on its own represents the first 20 per cent of the values. By referring to the First Loss Scale, we can see that the first 90 per cent of the risk is worth 95 per cent of the original premium. Therefore, we know that the premium for the cover plus the priority should be 95 per cent of the original premiums in that band of the profile. Also, we can see from the scale that the first 20 per cent of the risk is worth 66 per cent of the original premium. From this, we can deduce that 70 per cent excess of 20 per cent of the Sum Insured should be worth 29 per cent of the original premium.

We can perform this calculation for every band of the risk profile and for each of the layers. We can then total the reinsurance premiums for each band of the profile to arrive at a premium for the layer in question. However, as we have already seen, this premium is, in effect, nothing more than a total of facultative excess of loss premiums. If the per-risk excess of loss cover provided unlimited, free reinstatements, this would probably be a fair premium to pay, but in practice such contracts have limited reinstatements, which may sometimes be free, but are more usually subject to the payment of an additional premium. We therefore need to find a way to discount this "unlimited premium" to take into account this restriction upon the amount of cover provided.

3. Poisson Tables/Formula

Fortunately, statisticians have provided us with a useful tool for determining what the price of a cover should be if reinstatements are limited, and are subject to the payment of an additional premium. Poisson Tables are statistical calculations which say, for example, that if the probability of an event occurring an unlimited number of times is 80 per cent, the probability of it happening a first time is 57 per cent and the probability of it happening a second time is 19 per cent.

Some spreadsheet programmes, notably Microsoft Excel, have a built-in Poisson function. Unfortunately, Lotus 1-2-3 does not, and we need to derive the figures we need in two stages.

Firstly, in order to derive the cumulative Poisson, we use the formula:

@EXP(−C$17)*C$17 ∧ B18/@FACT(B18)

where cell C17 is the "Unlimited Rate on Line" and cell B18 is either a zero, meaning that it represents the first cover, or a whole number, representing the sequential number of the reinstatement. This formula will only work with Lotus 1-2-3 version 4 or higher, because lower versions do not support the Factorial function @FACT.

This formula firstly calculates the Exponential of the Unlimited Rate on Line and multiplies it by the Unlimited Rate on Line, raised to the power of the cover (0 for the first cover, 1 for the first reinstatement and so on), over the factorial of the reinstatement. This rather complex formula is difficult to understand, and I can only suggest that you read a textbook on advanced statistics. Alternatively, the Help file on the latest editions of Microsoft Excel provides some explanation of the Poisson function.

The above formula should be copied down for about six cells, in order to provide space for a decent number of reinstatements.

The above gives you a cumulative Poisson, from which we need to extract the individual elements to give us the cost of each successive cover (the first shall be the first cover, and subsequent calculations shall give us the respective reinstatement costs).

CONSTRUCTING THE PROPERTY RISK EXCESS RATING MODEL

In an ideal situation, we would like to see a risk profile with the aggregate sums insured and the numbers of risks in each band of values, as well as the premiums applicable to each band. This would enable an underwriter to make a judgement regarding the level of original rates being charged, so that, if this appears too low, he can adjust his quote accordingly.

However, for the purposes of this model, we shall only concern ourselves with the premiums, in order to keep things simple. This is the most complex spreadsheet we have covered so far, and if you are not familiar with spreadsheets, could be quite a challenge!

Actually, this model has three pages, which I have labelled "Profile", "Programme" and "Scale".

Starting with the Profile, this page actually contains most of the basic calculations. You can label it now by double clicking on the tab, or leave it as its default, "A". The Sum Insured Ranges can start at cell A14 and go down to B33 giving us 20 ranges. For example, A14 would have a cell value of 0 and cell B14 might have 1,000 representing the upper value of that range. How you divide the ranges depends upon the largest value in the profile and the proposed layering of the excess of loss programme. There is no point in having too many divisions at levels below the first layer priority, because none of these risks will expose the cover. On the other hand, if the divisions are too wide, it may not give an accurate view of the exposures into consecutive layers of the programme.

Column C will accept the total premium in each band of values. Column D simply calculates the mid-point of the value range, hence cell D14 will have the formula (A14+B14)/2 which is copied down as far as cell D33. The result of this calculation will be used in the calculation of other cells' values.

Profile

	A	B	C	D
	Minimum S/I	Maximum S/I	Gross Premiums	Mid-Point
13				
14	0	1,000	5,678	500
15	1,000	3,000	5,436	2,000
16	3,000	5,000	6,775	4,000
17	5,000	10,000	34,556	7,500
18	10,000	20,000	23,456	15,000
19	20,000	30,000	434,567	25,000
20	30,000	40,000	33,456	35,000
21	40,000	50,000	235,567	45,000
22	50,000	60,000	356,676	55,000
23	60,000	70,000	23,445	65,000
24	70,000	80,000	1,367	75,000
25	80,000	90,000	0	85,000
26	90,000	100,000	439	95,000
27	100,000	110,000	244	105,000
28	110,000	120,000	282	115,000
29	120,000	130,000	2,159	125,000
30	130,000	140,000	1,592	135,000

100 Excess of Loss Rating

Profile				
	A	B	C	D
31	140,000	150,000	0	145,000
32	150,000	160,000	171	155,000
33	160,000	200,000	13,398	180,000

Column E calculates the exposure to the layer, but before we can calculate it, we need to know the limit and priority of the proposed cover. We shall put the limit in cell F10 and the priority in F11. The labels can go into cells E10 and E11.

Profile		
	E	F
8		First Layer Calculations
9		
10	Cover	75,000
11	Deductible	25,000

Having entered some values for the limit and priority, we can now calculate how much each risk in a band exposes the cover. The formula is:

@IF($D14<=F$10,0,@IF($D14>=F$10+F$9,F$9,$D14−F$10)

which means that if the mid-point of the range is less than or equal to the priority of the cover, there is no exposure to the cover. Failing this, if the mid-point is greater than or equal to the sum of the limit and the priority, the cover limit is totally exposed, in other words, the exposure to the layer is equal to the monetary limit of the layer. Failing this, the mid-point is greater than the priority, and within the limit, so subtract the priority from the mid-point value of the range. This formula can be copied down as far as E33.

Profile	
	E
13	Exposure to Layer
14	0
15	0
16	0
17	0
18	0
19	0

Constructing the Property Risk Excess Rating Model

Profile	E
20	10,000
21	20,000
22	30,000
23	40,000
24	50,000
25	60,000
26	70,000
27	75,000
28	75,000
29	75,000
30	75,000
31	75,000
32	75,000
33	75,000

Column F expresses the values calculated in column E as percentages of the mid-point values in column D. We could use the simple formula: +E14/$D14* 100 and so on, down to cell F33. However, this can sometimes cause error values to appear, which creates problems throughout the spreadsheet. We therefore use the following:

@IF($D14<=F$10,0,@IF($D14>F$9+F$10,F$9/$D14* 100,($D14−F$10)/$D14*100))

Which means:

"If the mid-point is less than or equal to the priority, the percentage exposure is nil. If the mid-point is greater than the limit plus the priority, put the limit over the mid-point, as a percentage value. Failing both of these tests, the mid-point must have a value which exposes the layer, but not totally, so subtract the value of the priority from the value of the mid-point and express the result as a percentage of the mid-point."

In column G we are calculating the value of the priority as a percentage of the mid-point. For any mid-point value which is below the priority, we can say that the priority represents 100 per cent of the mid-point value (to have a figure greater than 100 per cent would be ridiculous, and would spoil the calculations). The formula for cell G14 is:

@IF(F$10>$D14,100,F$10/$D14*100)

which means that if the priority is greater than the mid-point, there is no exposure, so put 100 (meaning 100 per cent), otherwise put the value of the priority divided by the mid-point, times 100.

Profile	F Exposure as % of mid-point	G Priority as % of mid-point
13		
14	0	100
15	0	100
16	0	100
17	0	100
18	0	100
19	0	100
20	28.57	71.43
21	44.44	55.56
22	54.55	45.45
23	61.54	38.46
24	66.67	33.33
25	70.59	29.41
26	73.68	26.32
27	71.43	23.81
28	65.22	21.74
29	60	20
30	55.56	18.52
31	51.72	17.24
32	48.39	16.13
33	41.67	13.89

Column H calculates a rating factor, by referring to a First Loss Scale. In order to do this, we must first enter a First Loss Rating Scale. The scale you use can be derived from whatever source you choose. I have used a Lloyd's scale which has been in existence since about 1972, and which you will find reproduced in Appendix 4. I have only used whole numbers for the percentage of original values, even though the Lloyd's scale provides some fractional percentages. Create a new sheet and call it "Scale". I have entered the First Loss Amount in column A starting at cell A10 with a figure of 1 and going down to cell A109 in 1 per cent increments to end on 100 per cent. In column B we show the relevant Scale Rate, starting with 22.4 in cell B10. This means that if a first loss policy were to be issued covering 1 per cent of the total value at risk, the premium to be charged would be 22.4 per cent of the premium for a full value policy. The next stage is to highlight the figures in cells A10 to B109 (by holding the mouse button down and dragging over them) and to name the range, using *Range*, *Name* and then typing in a suitable name. By force of habit, I have named this range "DATA".

Going back to our Profile sheet, we can now write the formula for cell H14. The formula is a little more complex, because it relies on a lookup routine. First, here is the formula:

@VLOOKUP((F14+G14),$DATA,1)−
@VLOOKUP(G14,$DATA,1)

This is saying:

"Add the limit and priority percentages in cells F14 and G14 and look up the nearest number to it in the scale sheet, under column A. Then, read off the value one place to the right (the ',1' after DATA means 'offset one place to the right'). Next, look up the value nearest to the priority percentage in cell G14, and take the value one place to the right. Subtract the second figure from the first figure to give the answer."

Let us assume that the priority represents 20 per cent of the mid-point value, and the exposure to the layer represents 30 per cent. Together they account for the first 50 per cent of the value at risk, which requires 83 per cent of the original premium. The priority represents the first 20 per cent of the risk, requiring a premium of 65.5 per cent of the risk. Therefore 30 per cent excess of 20 per cent requires a premium of 17.5 per cent of the original premium. The reason we put a dollar sign in front of DATA is so that it does not alter the cell addresses when we copy the formula to other cells.

Column I calculates how much of the original premium should go to our proposed excess of loss cover. The formula for cell I14 is:

+$C14*H14/100

in other words the original premium for the band, times the rating factor for the exposure to the layer, divided by 100 (because the factor was multiplied by 100 to make it a percentage).

Profile		
	H	I
13	Rate Factor	Exposure Premium
14	0	0
15	0	0
16	0	0
17	0	0
18	0	0
19	0	0
20	12.4	4,149
21	16.1	37,926

104 Excess of Loss Rating

Profile		
	H	I
22	18.9	67,412
23	21.2	4,970
24	23	314
25	25.9	0
26	28	123
27	28.8	70
28	27	76
29	25.3	546
30	25.1	400
31	24.9	0
32	25.1	43
33	26.5	3,550

The figure we are looking to derive is the total premium due to the layer, in other words, the total from column I. I have put this figure in cell I38 with the simple formula:

@SUM(I14..I33)

Finally, for this sheet, we can calculate the so-called "Unlimited Rate on Line" in cell I9 which is just the total premium from cell I38, expressed as a percentage of the limit, hence: +I38/F9. This does not need to be multiplied by 100 as the Poisson formula uses decimal formatting, rather than percentages.

So far, we have put data into columns A, B and C. We have put calculations into columns D to I inclusive. For the sake of clarity, we are going to leave column J blank. We can make it narrower, and we can put a box around all of the calculations we have done so far. If we want to perform calculations for a further layer, we can simply copy everything from E9 down to I38 into a new block of cells starting at K9. Now, if we change the figures for the limit and deductible at cells L9 and L10 to reflect the terms of the second layer of the programme, the spreadsheet should do the rest.

In the final sheet, headed "Programme", we shall see how the calculated "Unlimited Rate on Line" should be adjusted to take account of the reinstatement terms of the contract.

Place a heading, "Subject GNPI" in cell A4, with the figure appearing in B4. Most contracts are rated on the Gross Net Premium Income of the protected account, even though the preliminary rating calculations use "Rate on Line". The contract limit and priority should appear in B8 and B9 respectively, with their headings in A8 and A9.

Constructing the Property Risk Excess Rating Model

Programme	A	B	C	D
4	Subject GNPI	43,000		
5		First Layer Rating Calculations		
6				Limited Free ROL
7				Reinst Cost
8	Limit	75,000		Contract ROL
9	Deductible	25,000		Rate on Income
10				To Earn
11	No. of Reinstatements	1		
12	Reinst. # 1 Cost	1	100%	79.70%
13	Reinst. # 2 Cost	0		0.00%
14	Reinst. # 3 Cost	0		0.00%
15	Reinst. # 4 Cost	0		0.00%
16	Reinst. # 5 Cost	0		0.00%
17	U'Ltd ROL		159.4401%	
18	Poisson	0	20.30%	
19	Poisson	1	32.37%	
20	Poisson	2	25.81%	
21	Poisson	3	13.72%	
22	Poisson	4	5.47%	
23	Poisson	5	1.74%	
24	Cover Cost	0	79.70%	
25	Cover Cost	1	47.33%	
26	Cover Cost	2	21.52%	
27	Cover Cost	3	7.80%	
28	Cover Cost	4	2.34%	
29	Cover Cost	5	0.59%	

Enter the number of reinstatements for the contract in B11 with its heading in A11. In the next five columns, we are going to calculate either a zero or a 1, depending upon the number of reinstatements. We can call the headings

"Reinstatement # 1 Cost" etc., from cells A12 to A16. In cell B12 we enter this simple formula:

@IF(B$11>0,1,0)

which we then copy down through to B16, but with one minor change; cell B13 will have the formula:

@IF(B$11>1,1,0)

cell B14 will look for a value in B11 greater than 2 and so on. This is like a "true or false" calculation, so that if the figure for the number of reinstatements is 5 (or greater), cells B12 to B16 will all have a value of 1. If the number of reinstatements is 4, cell B16 will have a value of zero, and so on.

Next comes the actual cost of the reinstatements as a percentage of the contract premium. These will go into cells C12 to C16 and will be entered as decimals. For example, if the cost of the first reinstatement is 100 per cent enter a 1 in cell C12. Cells C12 to C16 should be formatted as percentages, probably with the number of decimal places set to zero.

Cell A17 contains the heading "Unlimited Rate on Line" and its figure is placed in cell C17. This is a derived figure, and so its formula is:

+Profile:I9

Now we are going to break the Unlimited Rate on Line into its Poisson components. In cells A18 to A23 we have the simple heading "Poisson" and in B18 to B23 the numbers 0 to 5. In other words, we are calculating the Poisson for the first cover and the first five reinstatements. (If we wish to calculate a rate for a cover with more than five reinstatements, we can easily adapt the spreadsheet.)

In cells C18 to C23 we are going to calculate the Poisson for the first cover and subsequent reinstatements. In C18 we have the following formula:

@EXP(−C$17)*C$17^B18/@FACT(B18)

This should be copied down through to cell C23.

Please refer to the explanation already given in respect of this formula. The Poisson for each successive cover is not the actual rate which should be charged for that cover. We need to calculate the complementary of the cumulative Poisson, and we do this in cells C24 to C29 with the following formulae:

C24: 1-C18
C25: 1-@SUM(C18..C19)
C26: 1-@SUM(C18..C20)
C27: 1-@SUM(C18..C21)
C28: 1-@SUM(C18..C22)
C29: 1-@SUM(C18..C23)

As I am writing, the figure for the "Unlimited Rate on Line" in cell C17 is showing 159.4401 per cent. The corresponding Poisson components in cells C24 to C29 are:

- 79.70% for the first cover;
- 47.33% for the second cover (i.e. the first reinstatement);
- 21.52% for the second reinstatement;
- 7.80% for the third reinstatement;
- 2.34% for the fourth reinstatement;
- 0.59% for the fifth reinstatement.

Also, in my sample data, I have entered the number of reinstatements as 1 in cell B11 and the cost of the reinstatement as 1 (100 per cent) in C12.

In cells D12 to D16 we are going to calculate the cost of each reinstatement based upon the Poisson component of the Unlimited Rate on Line. This is simply a question of multiplying the Poisson components in cells C24 to C29 by the cost of the respective reinstatement in C12 to C16. Hence in cell D12 we have the formula +C24*C12 which we then copy down as far as D16.

In my data the figure currently displayed in D12 is 79.70 per cent being the Poisson value of the first cover, multiplied by 100 per cent which is the price of the first reinstatement.

The final calculations are a little complex, and are summarised below:

	D	E
6	Limited Free ROL	+C24+(C25*B12)+(C26*B13)+(C27*B14)+(C28*B15)+(C29*B16)
7	Reinst Cost	1+(C24*C12)+(C25*C13)+(C26*C14)+(C27*C15)+(C28*C16)
8	Contract ROL	+E6/E7
9	Rate on Income	+B8*E8/B4
10	To Earn	+B4*E9

In cell E6 we are calculating the sum of the Poisson rates for the first cover, plus any reinstatements. C24 is the first cover, C25 is the first reinstatement. B12 is either a 1 or a zero, depending upon whether or not there is a reinstatement. In my data, there is one reinstatement, so B12 is a 1. Cells B13 to B16 are all set to zero, because there are no subsequent reinstatements. Hence in my data, cell E6 computes to 127.02 per cent being the sum of 79.70 per cent and 47.33 per cent taken from cells C24 and C25.

The reinstatement cost is really an artificial calculation. In our spreadsheet, we are concerned with the Contract Rate on Line, which is represented by the Limited Free ROL over the Reinstatement Cost (hence the formula in cell E8 is +E6/E7).

The actual formula for calculating the Contract Rate on Line is:

108 Excess of Loss Rating

$$\frac{\text{Total of the Poisson rates for the cover and any reinstatements}}{1 + \text{the total cost of the reinstatements}}$$

Bear in mind that the cost of the first reinstatement is the percentage reinstatement cost applied to the Poisson cost of the first cover, not the reinstatement.

Having calculated the Contract Rate on Line, it is then a simple matter to convert this into a rate based upon the estimated Gross Net Premium Income (cell E9) and to estimate how much premium, in monetary terms, the contract will generate (cell E10).

Programme		
	D	E
6	Limited Free ROL	127.02%
7	Reinst Cost	179.70%
8	Contract ROL	70.69%
9	Rate on Income	123.29%
10	To Earn	53,015

For rating subsequent layers, we can simply copy the entire cell range from A5 to E29, leaving a single column gap between the layers. Hence the second layer calculations can be pasted into cell G5. This will ensure that all of the calculations will refer to the correct cells in the spreadsheet.

That completes the Risk Excess of Loss Rating Model. I hope you will find it useful, but I do urge you not to take the results as Gospel. I must stress that this is only one way of calculating rates, and underwriters may build in many other factors, such as original acquisition costs, adequacy (or otherwise) of original rates, reinsurance brokerage etc., as well as commercial considerations.

CATASTROPHE RATING

Another statistical tool used in excess of loss rating is a type of frequency distribution known as "Pareto". This is the most common way of rating catastrophe excess of loss contracts, in order to ensure consistency in rating across an entire catastrophe programme. If an underwriter has calculated the rate for a particular layer of cover, other layers of the same programme can be rated by "reading off" the rate from a suitable Pareto Curve. "Suitable" refers to the fact that Pareto Curves, like all statistical curves, can be derived from a mathematical formula, which has a variable factor. The size of the variable depends upon the observed loss patterns for the type of business or territory being studied.

In the absence of "suitable" Pareto Curves, we can make a very rough guess at the rating for a catastrophe programme, using the same first loss scale as was used in the Risk Excess of Loss Rating Model.

Essentially, all we are going to do is establish the correct premium or loss cost for the catastrophe PML, and then apply our First Loss Scale to this figure. However, there are several stages we need to go through first:

Stage 1—Index the claims history

Hopefully, there will be some sort of claims history for the perils concerned. We should be very careful when looking at the previous claims history, as certain key factors may have changed. For example, the Reinsured may have stopped granting earthquake cover as an automatic extension, and may now only grant cover by special endorsement, at an additional premium. Another good example concerns policy deductibles; in the Caribbean area, windstorm deductibles were hardly ever applied before the advent of Hurricane Hugo. Since then, deductibles of 2 per cent of insured value have been commonplace. If such deductibles had been applied before Hugo, the insured losses would have been considerably less.

Indexation of the claims should take into account not only inflation, but the growth in the protected account. This can be achieved by indexing based upon the growth in the Reinsured's premium income (the GNPI). For example, if the GNPI in 1990 was $20 million when a catastrophe loss of $5 million was suffered, and in 1995 the GNPI had grown to $30 million the $5 million loss could be indexed to $7.5 million. Assuming that rates have not changed, the increase in the GNPI should reflect inflation plus the growth in the Reinsured's business.

Stage 2—Establish the catastrophe PML

This may be the same as the total amount of cover, including deductible, which the Reinsured is purchasing. It is for this reason that underwriters often stipulate in their quotations "warranted no higher layer carried". In other words, the underwriter, in preparing his quotation, has taken the amount of cover purchased as the Reinsured's assessment of the catastrophe PML. Should the Reinsured subsequently decide to purchase more cover, it can be deduced that his estimation of the PML has increased. Consequently, the reinsurer can be thought to be more heavily exposed, and may wish to charge a higher premium.

As an alternative to establishing the PML in this way, we can turn to market information, such as that supplied by the CRESTA organisation, which may suggest the PML for various catastrophe perils, as a percentage of the protected aggregate sum insured.

Stage 3—Calculate the "as if" loss experience

Having indexed the losses, we can then take the largest loss as a guide, and work out the "as if" losses for a fictitious layer of 90 per cent excess of 10 per cent of the largest loss. Hence if our largest indexed loss is $40 million, we have a fictitious layer of $36 million excess of $4 million. We can then apply these limits to all of the indexed loss amounts, to arrive at the as if loss position for that layer. These as if losses should then be totalled and divided by the number of years in the observation.

Stage 4—Calculate the fictitious limit and deductible as percentages of the PML

For example, if the catastrophe PML is $80 million a layer of $36 million excess of $4 million represents 45 per cent excess of 5 per cent of the PML.

Stage 5—Find a loss factor from the First Loss Scale

In our 45 per cent excess of 5 per cent example, we are saying that we are covering up to 50 per cent of the PML. From our First Loss Scale, the rate for the first 50 per cent of cover is 83 per cent. The rate for the first 5 per cent is 42.5 per cent and so it is logical to assume that the rate for 45 per cent excess of 5 per cent should be 83 − 42.5 per cent or 40.5 per cent. If we now take the average as if loss for the 45 per cent excess of 5 per cent layer and divide it by this loss factor, we will arrive at the 100 per cent loss cost. In other words, if the average as if loss is $10 million the 100 per cent loss cost would be $10 million/.405 = $24,691,358.

Stage 6—Establish the proposed limit and priority as percentages of the PML

A layer with a limit of $20 million excess of $20 million protecting a PML of $80 million has a limit of 25 per cent excess of 25 per cent of the PML.

Stage 7—Apply First Loss Scale to the 100 per cent loss cost

The layer 25 per cent excess of 25 per cent takes us up to the first 50 per cent of the PML. We have established that the loss cost (or pure risk premium) as $24,691,358 in our example. The first 50 per cent of cover, according to our First Loss Scale, accounts for 83 per cent of the premium. The first 25 per cent (the deductible or priority) accounts for 71.2 per cent of the premium. We can therefore deduce that the premium for 25 per cent excess of 25 per cent would require 11.8 per cent of the pure risk premium, equivalent to

$2,913,580. This figure may then be expressed as a percentage of the GNPI for contract rating purposes.

Please note that this is a very rough guide. Every reinsurer will have a different method of calculating rates. Many will load the rate by a so-called "Fluctuation Loading" to protect themselves against early occurrences of catastrophes, or losses of such a magnitude as to defy previous predictions. Also, care needs to be taken when dealing with an account protecting multiple perils and multiple catastrophe zones. Nevertheless, it should prove useful as a rough guide to estimating rates, provided it is used judiciously, and modified for local circumstances.

CONSTRUCTING A CATASTROPHE RATING MODEL

For this simple model, we are going to use the same spreadsheet file that contains the Risk Excess of Loss Rating Model. Open it now and click on the box in the toolbar, headed "New Sheet".

First of all, we shall put in some basic data. The headings "GNPI", "PML", "Limit", "Deductible" and "Index" can go into cells A2 to A6 with their figures appearing alongside, in the corresponding rows of column B. The figure for Index should be the current index figure, as explained above.

Catastrophe				
1	A	B	C	D
2				
3	GNPI	16,000,000		Rating Factor
4	PML	80,000,000	% of PML	11.5
5	Limit	20,000,000	25	Rate on GNPI
6	Deductible	20,000,000	25	
7	Index		150	
8			Loss Statistics	
9		Year	Index	Amount	Indexed Amount
10		1990	100	3,000,000	4,500,000
11		1991	115	750,000	978,261
12		1992	120	500,000	625,000
13		1993	130	9,793,333	11,300,000
14		1994	135	0	0
15		1995	150	40,000,000	40,000,000

Excess of Loss Rating

Catastrophe				
	A	B	C	D
16				
17				Average
18	Factor			
19	on Loss	40.2		
20	Loss Cost	18,159,204		

In cells A8 to E8 we can put the headings "Year", "Index", "Amount", "Indexed Amount" and "As if 90% XS 10%". The "Amount" column represents the amount of each individual catastrophe loss. If there were two catastrophe losses in a single year, you would need to enter both figures. Do *not* add the catastrophe claims for one year together. "Indexed Amount", starting in cell D9, has the formula +C9*$B$6/B9 which may then be copied down as far as necessary (I have taken mine down to row 14 for simplicity's sake). The "As if 90% XS 10%" column works out the losses for a fictitious layer of 90 per cent excess of 10 per cent of the largest indexed loss. It contains the formula:

@IF(D9>$F$6,D9 – $F$6,0)

This means that if the indexed amount is less than 10 per cent of the largest indexed loss, put zero, otherwise, calculate the indexed loss, less the deductible. The only problem is, cell F6 is blank at the moment, so this calculation will produce the result "ERR". To correct this, let us now calculate the cover and deductible of the fictitious 90 per cent excess of 10 per cent layer. In cells E5 and E6 enter the headings "90% Largest Loss" and "10% Largest Loss". The calculations in cells F5 and F6 are:

@MAX(D9..D14)*0.9 and
@MAX(D9..D14)*0.1

In other words, find the maximum figure from the range of cells D9 to D14 and multiply it by 90 per cent to arrive at the limit and by 10 per cent to arrive at the deductible.

Catastrophe				
	D	E	F	G
1				
2	Rating Factor	Premium		
3	11.5	2,088,308		
4	Rate on GNPI	13.05		As % of PML
5		90% Largest Loss	36,000,000	45
6		10% Largest Loss	4,000,000	5

Catastrophe				
	D	E	F	G
7				
8	Indexed Amount	As if 90% XS 10%		
9	4,500,000	500,000		
10	978,261	0		
11	625,000	0		
12	11,300,000	7,300,000		
13	0	0		
14	40,000,000	36,000,000		
15		43,800,000		
16	Average	7,300,000		

Now that we have calculated the fictitious cover and deductible, we should express these as percentages of the catastrophe PML. In cell G5 we can use the formula:

+F5/$B$3*100

Cell G6 is a little more tricky, because we want to avoid error values which may occur later if the figure for 10 per cent of the largest loss computes to less than 1. We therefore use the following formula:

@IF(F6/$B$3*100)<1,1,F6/$B$3*100)

This is because our First Loss Scale does not contain any figures below 1 per cent.

The as if losses may now be totalled in cell E15 with the formula:

@SUM(E9..E14)

and an average may be calculated in cell E16 using the formula:

+E15/@COUNT(E9..E14)

This is dividing the average as if loss by the number of years. Note that if you have more than one catastrophe loss in any year, you need to modify this formula; if not, you will end up dividing by the number of losses, which will give a false result.

The next job is to calculate the factor to be applied to the as if average loss. In our example, we are looking at a fictitious layer for 45 per cent excess of 5 per cent of the PML. As we have already seen, this requires a premium of 40.5 per cent of the Pure Risk Premium. However, we are going to use the "@VLOOKUP" function in Lotus 1-2-3 and this produces a minor anomaly. If we are looking up a figure of 45 in the table, and Lotus cannot find exactly

45, it will take the next lowest value, rather than the nearest value. Sometimes, the cell whose value you wish to look up may appear to contain a value of 45, but internally, Lotus may recognise it as 44.9999. This may cause Lotus to return the value from the lookup table corresponding to 44, rather than 45. The errors this produces are usually not serious, but it helps to be aware of them, because it means that you will sometimes see slightly different results from those at which you would arrive at by manual calculation. The calculation of the factor is carried out in cell B18 with the formula:

> @VLOOKUP((G5+G6),$DATA,1) − @VLOOKUP(G6,$DATA,1)

To prove a point, my example of 45 per cent excess of 5 per cent has returned a factor of 40.2 rather than 40.5.

The value from cell B18 is then used to "gross up" the as if losses to a notional 100 per cent value. In other words, we are saying:

> "If a contract for 45 per cent excess of 5 per cent of the current catastrophe PML would have produced average losses over a given period of $7,300,000, and if we know that 45 per cent excess of 5 per cent represents (statistically speaking) 40.2 per cent of all losses, then 100 per cent of all losses (averaged over a period) would be around $18,159,204 (the loss cost, or pure risk premium)."

We calculate this in cell B19 with the formula:

> +E16/B18*100

Now, all we need to do to calculate the premium for our layer is to apply the First Loss Rating Scale to the Pure Risk Premium, which can be done as follows.

In cell D3 we calculate the rating factor for our layer. We have already established in cells C4 and C5 that the Limit and Deductible in our example each represent 25 per cent of the PML. We therefore need the formula:

> @VLOOKUP((C4+C5),$DATA,1) − @VLOOKUP(C5,$DATA,1)

This will return a value of 11.5 for our example. In cell E3 we can apply this factor to the Pure Risk Premium to arrive at a premium for the contract, using:

> +B19*D3/100

Finally, we can convert this premium into a rate on GNPI in cell E4 using:

> +E3/B2*100

That completes our simple rating model, which you can hopefully modify to suit your individual needs.

CHAPTER 8

MARKET EVOLUTION

Reinsurance is a constantly evolving business, and as our world grows more complex, the potential for greater financial losses is growing at an alarming rate.

Although it is the job of underwriters to foresee the likeliest causes of major losses, it is true to say that the insurance/reinsurance community is often caught unawares by the scale and nature of losses, and is sometimes forced to change direction in the light of expensive experience.

For example, prior to Hurricane Tracy in Darwin in 1974 it was possible to purchase per-risk excess of loss covers with unlimited reinstatements. This meant that although reinsurers placed strict limits upon the amount of loss they could sustain on a single risk, they carried potentially unlimited liability with regard to the number of individual losses the contract could sustain in a single event. Nowadays it is unlikely that such covers could be placed. Reinsurers impose limited reinstatements on property risk excess of loss contracts, and may also impose separate limits per event.

Another example was the oil rig explosion on Piper Alpha in the North Sea. Prior to this event, it was normal for employers to purchase unlimited Employers' Liability coverage. These days, due to the non-availability of reinsurance protection, insurers in the UK only offer liability coverage of up to £10 million per employer, although there is a small market for excess of loss insurance above that figure.

In the area of property covers, reinsurers have recently become acutely aware of some unusual weather patterns. The UK and other parts of Northern Europe were affected by a hurricane in 1987, and severe storms in 1990. The 1980s and 1990s have witnessed severe weather-related losses virtually all over the globe, whilst earthquake losses now have a greater potential for economic loss, due to increasing industrialisation and insurance awareness. This has led reinsurers to attempt to limit their liability under proportional property treaties, by imposing per-event limitations. In some ways, this is a similar measure to the post-Darwin event limitations under per-risk excess of loss covers. However, there is one important difference. An excess of loss cover is rated to some degree independently of original premiums, because the reinsurer is not participating in the losses to the same degree as the Reinsured. In proportional reinsurance, on the other hand, the reinsurers are receiving the same share of the original premium on each risk that they should pay in respect of any losses. It therefore seems cynical of the reinsurers to try to limit their share of a catastrophe loss to less than their true share, based upon the proportion of the original premiums which they have received.

Reinsurers may argue that they cannot accept unlimited liability, but in reality, this is precisely what the Ceding Company is doing all of the time. The liability of the reinsurers for their share of a treaty is no more unlimited than the potential liability of the Ceding Company on the totality of its retained shares. The Ceding Company must assess its retained liabilities and try to estimate the amount of catastrophe protection required to protect it against the worst foreseeable loss situation. The reinsurer must attempt to do the same, but bearing in mind that the reinsurer is accepting treaties and facultative risks from all over the world. The calculations are therefore more complex, and some reinsurers have been finding that the profits earned from reinsurance are sometimes not sufficient to allow them to purchase adequate levels of catastrophe protection; hence their attempts to reduce potential liabilities whilst maintaining premium volume.

An alternative to catastrophe event limits in proportional property treaties is to limit the amount of business ceded to the treaty in respect of a single catastrophe zone. For example, the total amount of sum insured ceded in respect of risks located in Mexico City must not exceed a stipulated figure at any time during the life of the contract. Provided the Reinsured is careful not to exceed these limits, the reinsurers will always be providing catastrophe coverage up to the full extent of their share of each individual risk. If at the time of a catastrophe loss, it is found that the limits for the affected zone have been exceeded, the reinsurers will be entitled to apply the condition of Average to the whole loss occurrence, and reduce their payment accordingly.

These are just a few examples of ways in which the reinsurance market has adapted its practices in the light of experience. There are of course many more, including asbestosis and the mounting costs of litigation in the United States.

CHAPTER 9

OVER TO YOU

Whether you are new to the reinsurance industry or a seasoned professional, I hope that you have gained something from this book. It is by no means intended to be an exhaustive reference work, but rather a collection of ideas, upon which you can build.

One thing which is certain is that we never stop learning. The insurance industry deals with many facets of the risk business, and employs specialists in many fields, all of them building upon a vast wealth of knowledge and experience, and adapting to suit the needs of a rapidly changing world. My own career in reinsurance has been somewhat generalist. Even so, hardly a day goes by when I do not learn something new, or at least gain a fresh insight into some aspect of the job I had previously taken for granted.

Increasingly, science and mathematics are coming to play in the reinsurance industry. The traditional role of the reinsurance broker as a finder of capacity is being swept away by the communications revolution, and in order to survive we must now place a much greater emphasis upon providing professional and independent advice. This bodes well for those who are willing and able to take up the challenge of learning new skills, and should ensure plenty of job satisfaction for tomorrow's reinsurance professional.

CONTACT ME

If you have any comments or suggestions regarding this book, I would be pleased to hear from you. My Compuserve address is: 100752,1507

APPENDIX 1

ANSWERS TO PRACTICAL EXERCISE 1

DISTRIBUTION OF PREMIUMS AND CLAIMS OVER A PROPORTIONAL PROGRAMME

1. From the Table of Retentions, we can see that the company can take 100 per cent of its maximum retention for this risk. The distribution is therefore as follows:

	Sum Insured	%	Premium	Claim
Retention	300,000	1.2	600	420
Quota Share	700,000	2.8	1,400	980
1st Surplus	10,000,000	40	20,000	14,000
2nd Surplus	10,000,000	40	20,000	14,000
Fac. Oblig.	4,000,000	16	8,000	5,600
Facultative	0	0	0	0

2. From the Table of Retentions, we can see that the company can take 50 per cent of its maximum retention for this risk. The distribution is therefore as follows:

	Sum Insured	%	Premium	Claim
Retention	150,000	0.75	435	292.5
Quota Share	350,000	1.75	1,015	682.5
1st Surplus	5,000,000	25	14,500	9,750
2nd Surplus	5,000,000	25	14,500	9,750
Fac. Oblig.	9,500,000	47.5	27,550	18,525
Facultative	0	0	0	0

Answers to Practical Exercise 1

3. From the Table of Retentions, we can see that the company can take 60 per cent of its maximum retention for this risk. The distribution is therefore as follows:

	Sum Insured	%	Premium	Claim
Retention	180,000	1.2	456	4,200
Quota Share	420,000	2.8	1,064	9,800
1st Surplus	6,000,000	40	15,200	140,000
2nd Surplus	6,000,000	40	15,200	140,000
Fac. Oblig.	2,400,000	16	6,080	56,000
Facultative	0	0	0	0

4. From the Table of Retentions, we can see that the company can take 70 per cent of its maximum retention for this risk. The distribution is therefore as follows:

	Sum Insured	%	Premium	Claim
Retention	210,000	1.17	420	175
Quota Share	490,000	2.72	980	408.33
1st Surplus	7,000,000	38.89	14,000	5,833.33
2nd Surplus	7,000,000	38.89	14,000	5,833.33
Fac. Oblig.	3,300,000	18.33	6,600	2,750
Facultative	0	0	0	0

It should be noted that the company is *not* obliged to cede to the Facultative Obligatory Cover, and could choose to place some of the risk facultatively, after using its quota share and surplus treaties.

APPENDIX 2

ANSWERS TO PRACTICAL EXERCISE 2

PROFIT COMMISSION CALCULATIONS

Exercise 2(a)

Income

Premiums ceded:	428,394
Premium portfolio entry at 40%	139,171
Outstanding loss entry at 90%	86,206
Total of income:	653,771

Outgo

Commission at 35%	149,938
Paid losses:	104,346
Premium portfolio withdrawal at 40%	171,358
Outstanding loss withdrawal at 90%	59,388
Reinsurers' expenses at 5%	21,420
Total of outgo	506,450
Income	653,771
Profit for year:	147,321
Deficit c/f from previous year	66,933
Final profit:	80,388
Profit commission at 25%	20,097

Exercise 2(b)
Year 1
Income

Premiums ceded:	348,540

Outgo

Commission at 35%	121,989
Paid losses:	124,678
Premium portfolio withdrawal at 40%	139,436
Outstanding loss withdrawal at 90%	92,839
Reinsurers' expenses at 7.5%	26,141
Total of outgo	505,083
Income	348,540
Deficit	156,543

Year 2
Income

Premiums ceded:	347,928
Premium portfolio entry at 40%	139,436
Outstanding loss entry at 90%	92,839
Total of income:	580,203

Outgo

Commission at 35%	121,775
Paid losses:	134,759
Premium portfolio withdrawal at 40%	139,171
Outstanding loss withdrawal at 90%	86,206
Reinsurers' expenses at 7.5%	26,095
Total of outgo	508,006
Income	580,203
Profit for year	72,197
Deficit c/f from previous year	146,543
Final deficit:	74,346

Year 3

Income

Premiums ceded:	428,394
Premium portfolio entry at 40%	139,171
Outstanding loss entry at 90%	86,206
Total of income:	653,771

Outgo

Commission at 35%	149,938
Paid losses:	104,346
Premium portfolio withdrawal at 40%	171,358
Outstanding loss withdrawal at 90%	59,388
Reinsurers' expenses at 7.5%	32,130
Total of outgo	517,160
Income	653,771
Profit for year:	136,611
Deficit c/f from previous year	74,347
Final profit:	62,264
Profit commission at 25%	15,566

APPENDIX 3

ANSWERS TO PRACTICAL EXERCISE 3

EXCESS OF LOSS CLAIMS ALLOCATIONS

The period for a freeze loss is 168 hours, or seven days.
The first task is to deduct the recoveries from the per-risk covers, which operate in excess of $250,000 each loss, each risk. There were two losses of $400,000 each and one of $300,000.

All of these losses occurred in 1995. There will be the following recoveries under the 1995 per-risk programme:

Loss	$400,000	400,000	300,000
Priority	$250,000	250,000	250,000
Recovery	$150,000	150,000	50,000

The reinstatement premiums will be calculated as follows:

Loss # 1: $150,000/750,000 \times 120,000 \times 100\% = 24,000$
Loss # 2: $150,000/750,000 \times 120,000 \times 100\% = 24,000$
Loss # 3: $50,000/750,000 \times 120,000 \times 100\% = 8,000$

The above three losses are now shown for net amounts of $250,000 each.

We then need to total the losses for each day from the start of the event, and list the days in order. We must be careful to list all of the days, even if there were no recorded losses on some of them. This will enable us to take running totals of the losses from various periods of seven consecutive days.

A spreadsheet programme, such as Lotus 1-2-3 or Microsoft Excel is an ideal tool for performing these calculations.

Bear in mind that the object is not necessarily to maximise the Ultimate Net Loss, but to maximise the company's benefit from the programme. In this case, it was only necessary to compare two possible solutions, as follows:

Answers to Practical Exercise 3

DATE	NET LOSS	7 DAYS	7 DAYS
28/12/94	20,000		
29/12/94	50,000		
30/12/94	70,000		
31/12/94	100,000		
01/01/95	0		
02/01/95	460,000		
03/01/95	80,000	780,000	
04/01/95	450,000		1,210,000
05/01/95	0		
06/01/95	50,000		
07/01/95	100,000		
08/01/95	70,000		
09/01/95	70,000		
10/01/95	250,000	990,000	
11/01/95	120,000		
12/01/95	50,000	170,000	710,000
UNL		1,940,000	1,920,000
No. of occurrences		3	2

If we choose to start the first seven-day period on day 1, the ultimate net loss is $1,940,000 but the company would have to bear three priorities under the catastrophe programme. On the other hand, if we ignore day 1 as well as day 9, we arrive at a slightly smaller ultimate net loss, but the company now only has to pay two priorities under the catastrophe programme.

Therefore, the catastrophe programme would operate as follows:

First event:

Date of loss:	29/12/94	
Ultimate net loss	1,210,000	
1st layer recovery	650,000	Reinstatement premium 40,000
2nd layer recovery	210,000	Reinstatement premium 10,500

Second event:

Date of loss:	06/01/94	
Ultimate net loss	710,000	
1st layer recovery	360,000	Reinstatement premium 24,396

APPENDIX 4

SPECIMEN SCALE OF PROPERTY FIRST LOSS RATES

1st loss amount	Scale Rate	1st loss amount	Scale Rate	1st loss amount	Scale Rate
1	22.4	34	77.3	68	86.9
2	28.1	35	77.6	69	87.1
3	31	36	78	70	87.3
4	36.7	37	78.4	71	87.6
5	42.5	38	78.8	72	87.8
6	44.8	39	79.2	73	88
7	47.1	40	79.5	74	88.3
8	49.2	41	79.9	75	88.5
9	51.7	42	80.2	76	89
10	54	43	80.4	77	89.4
11	55.1	44	80.8	78	89.9
12	56.3	45	81.1	79	90.6
13	57.4	46	81.5	80	90.8
14	58.6	47	81.8	81	91.3
15	59.7	48	82.1	82	91.7
16	60.9	49	82.4	83	92.2
17	62	50	82.7	84	92.6
18	63.2	51	83	85	93.1
19	64.3	52	83.2	86	93.6
20	65.5	53	83.4	87	94
21	66.6	54	83.7	88	94.5
22	67.8	55	83.9	89	94.9
23	68.9	56	84.1	90	95.4
24	70.1	57	84.4	91	95.9
25	71.2	58	84.6	92	96.3
26	72	59	84.8	93	96.8
27	72.7	60	85	94	97.2
28	73.4	61	85.3	95	97.7
29	74.1	62	85.5	96	98.2
30	74.8	63	85.7	97	98.6
31	75.6	64	86	98	99.1
32	76.3	65	86.2	99	99.5
33	77	66	86.4	100	100
		67	86.7		

APPENDIX 5

SPECIMEN TREATY WORDINGS

NON MARINE SURPLUS TREATY

REINSURANCE AGREEMENT

made and entered into between

———

(hereinafter referred to as the "Reinsured")

of the one part

and

INSURANCE AND REINSURANCE COMPANIES

Whose signatures appear on the Signing Schedules attached hereto each for their one part and not one for the other

(hereinafter referred to as the "Reinsurers")

of the other part

WHEREBY IT IS AGREED AS FOLLOWS:

Article 1: Reinsuring Clause

The Reinsured agrees to cede and the Reinsurers agree to accept by way of reinsurance a share of business, whether direct or as coinsurance or by way of facultative reinsurance, underwritten by the Reinsured, as set out in the Schedule attached to and forming part of this Agreement on risks situated in {COUNTRY} including their interests abroad except for Personal Accident, Cash in Transit, Personal Effects and Travel Insurance which may be situated Worldwide.

Article 2: Exclusions

It is agreed that this Agreement shall not cover:

(i) Any liability assumed by Reinsured on loss or damage directly or indirectly occasioned by, happening through or in consequence of war, invasion, acts of foreign enemies, hostilities or war-like operations (whether war be declared or not), civil war, mutiny, civil commotion assuming the proportions of or amounting to a popular rising, military rising, insurrection, rebellion, revolution, military or usurped power, martial law, confiscation or nationalisation or requisition or destruction of or damage to property by or under the order of any Government or public or local authority.

However, it is agreed that, the foregoing paragraph shall not apply to those classes of business which are written in accordance with the War and Civil War Exclusion Agreement and the War and Civil War Exclusion Agreement nor to business outside the scope of those Agreements unless such classes of business are not covered by this Agreement.

This Agreement does not cover any liability assumed by the Reinsured on loss or damage directly or indirectly occasioned by, happening through or in consequence of any act of any person or persons acting on behalf of or in connection with any organisation the objects of which are to include the overthrowing or influencing of any *de jure* or *de facto* government by terrorism or by any violent means.

(ii) Nuclear Energy Risks as per Nuclear Energy Risks Exclusion Clause (1994) NMA 1975a (as attached).

(iii) Obligatory reinsurances.

(iv) Pro Rata Treaty reinsurances and all forms of Excess of Loss reinsurances other than Coinsurance and Facultative reinsurances from local market.

(v) Permanent Accident and Sickness.

(vi) Bonds (other than Bankers Blanket), Financial Guarantees and Penalties.

(vii) Marine and Off-shore Technology Risks.

(viii) Third Party Liability in respect of Contractor's Plant and Equipment whilst being driven under its own power on the public highway.

(ix) Deterioration of Stock in respect of Machinery Breakdown Section.

(x) Advanced Loss of Profits.

(xi) Decennale Covers.

(xii) Satellite Risks.

Article 3: Conditions

The liability of the Reinsurers for amounts ceded to them under this Agreement commences simultaneously with that of the Reinsured and shall be identical in every way with that of the Reinsured. An insurance effected by the Reinsured wherein the Reinsured is named as the Insured either alone or jointly with another party, shall be deemed to be an insurance coming within the scope of this Agreement notwithstanding that no legal liability may arise in respect thereof by reason of the fact, that the Reinsured is named as the Insured or one of the Insureds. All cessions hereunder shall be subject to the same clauses and conditions as the original policies, except in so far as they are contrary to the terms of this Agreement. The Reinsurers agree to follow the settlements of the Reinsured and pay as may be paid by them it being understood that the intention of this Agreement is that the Reinsurers shall follow the fortunes of the Reinsured in all respects.

The Reinsured shall have absolute discretion in fixing the amount of its retention on any one risk and in determining what constitutes one risk.

Nothing contained in this Agreement to the contrary will prevent the Reinsured from revising the amount of its retention provided it has no knowledge of the risk having been affected by a loss.

This Agreement shall be subject where applicable to the provisions of the Special Conditions, if any, embodied in the attached Schedule.

Long term risks to be ceded for a period of 12 months at a time other than CAR/EAR risks.

The Reinsured may submit to the Reinsurers for their consideration details of any risk falling outside the scope of this Agreement, and if accepted by the Reinsurers, such risks shall be considered as coming within the scope of this Agreement.

Article 4: Registers of Risks

The Reinsured shall keep at their office registers in which shall be entered all risks ceded hereunder. An entry in such a register constitutes a cession hereunder and shall be binding upon Reinsurers.

In the event of the Reinsured sustaining a loss before an entry has been made in such a register, the Reinsured shall nevertheless be entitled to claim from the Reinsurers in accordance with the provisions of this Agreement.

Article 5: Bordereaux and Inspection of Records

The Reinsured shall not be required to furnish bordereaux to the Reinsurers.

It is however understood and agreed that the Reinsurers hereon or their duly authorised representatives, shall have the right to inspect the books of the Reinsured on all matters pertaining to this Agreement at all reasonable times and upon reasonable notice being given. It is agreed that the Reinsurers' rights of inspection shall continue as long as either party has a claim against the other arising out of this Agreement.

Article 6: Premium

The premium payable to the Reinsurers under this Agreement shall be a proportionate share of the original gross premiums received by the Reinsured in respect of the business covered hereunder, less only the Reinsurers' proportion of any cancellations or returns of premium.

The Reinsurers shall pay to the Reinsured upon the gross premiums defined above commission at the rates specified in the Schedule. The Reinsurers shall also bear their proportion of any taxes for which the Reinsured may be liable to the extent specified in the Schedule.

Article 7: Profit Commission

The Reinsurers shall allow the Reinsured a profit commission on the Combined Results of Fire, Miscellaneous Accident, Renewable Engineering, Contractors All Risks and Erection All Risks Sections at the rate specified in the Schedule on the actual net profit to the Reinsurers for each underwriting year. Such profit commission shall be calculated on the dates specified in the Schedule for each underwriting year, in accordance with the following formula:

Income

(1) Losses outstanding from the previous profit commission statement for the underwriting year under consideration.
(2) Gross premiums for the current year as defined in Article 6.
(3) Premium reserve brought forward from the previous profit commission statement for the underwriting year under consideration.

Outgo

(1) Commission, taxes and other charges if applicable as defined in Article 6 calculated on item (2) of Income.
(2) Losses and loss expenses paid during the current year on business falling within the underwriting year under consideration.
(3) Losses outstanding at the end of the current year for the underwriting year under consideration.
(4) Premium reserve at the end of the current year in accordance with Article 10 calculated on item (2) of Income.
(5) Reinsurers' management expenses calculated at the percentage specified in the Schedule.
(6) Deficit, if any, carried forward from the previous underwriting year(s) of Account.

The excess of INCOME over OUTGO, calculated as above, represents the net profit upon which the profit commission shall be paid.

Should the transactions of any underwriting year result in a loss for any profit sharing period, the total amount of such loss shall appear as a further item of Outgo in the profit sharing account of the ensuing year or years for a maximum of five further underwriting years unless such loss is extinguished by subsequent profit before this five-year period has elapsed.

In the event of this Agreement being terminated in accordance with the Special Cancellation provisions of Article 12 no further profit commission shall be payable until all liability hereunder has been determined.

It shall be noted that the first Profit Commission Statement shall be calculated at {EXPIRY DATE} and to be annually adjusted thereafter until all liabilities under the underwriting year under consideration have been extinguished and deficits under any of the preceding {NUMBER OF YEARS OF DEFICIT CARRY FORWARD} underwriting years profit commission calculations have been finally established.

Article 8: Claims Settlements

All settlements, compromises and expenses including *ex gratia* payments, in consequence of losses on business ceded under this Agreement will be under the sole management and discretion of the Reinsured which will be at liberty to commence, defend, compromise, settle or withdraw from legal actions, suits and prosecutions and adopt any other means in connection with the adjustment of claims as it may think fit.

The Reinsurer will be liable for its share of the claim and all costs and expenses incurred in connection therewith excluding office expenses and salaries of officials of the Reinsured but the Reinsurer will be entitled to its share of any salvages or recoveries relating to such claim.

All losses shall be dealt with in the accounts provided for in Article 9, but in the event of the Reinsured sustaining a loss to this Agreement in excess of the amount specified in the Schedule under the heading "Cash Loss" the Reinsurers shall pay their proportion of the claim immediately in cash, if so requested by the Reinsured. It is understood, however, that any balances due in favour of the Reinsurers at the time of such a request for a cash settlement, may first be deducted from the amount of the claim.

The Reinsurers shall have the right to inspect at the offices of the Reinsured all original documents relating to any loss, without however refusing or delaying payment on their part of such loss and/or expenses.

Article 9: Accounts

The accounts hereunder shall be compiled at the dates specified in the Schedule, and shall be rendered by the Reinsured to the Reinsurers as soon as possible, but not later than eight weeks after the close of each accounting period.

The accounts shall be rendered in the main currency specified in the Schedule and other currencies shall be converted at the same rate of exchange at which they were remitted to or paid by the Reinsured or failing this, at the rates of exchange ruling on the last day of the month in which the relative account was compiled.

The accounts shall be rendered on an underwriting year basis, broken down between Fire, Accident and Car/Machinery Breakdown branches.

The accounts shall be confirmed by the Reinsurers within 30 days after their receipt and the balance on either side shall be paid within 30 days after receipt of such confirmation.

It is agreed that either party may deduct from any balance due to the other party any sum owing by the latter to the former whether under this Agreement or any other Treaty Agreement between the parties hereto.

Article 10: Premium Reserve and Interest

The Reinsured shall be entitled to retain as Premium Reserve a percentage, as specified by local legislation and mentioned in the Schedule, of the premium credited to the Reinsurer in each quarterly account. This reserve shall be retained by the Reinsured for 12 months and released to the Reinsurer in the account for the corresponding quarter of the following year. The Reinsured shall pay to the Reinsurers on such Reserve Fund interest at the rate specified in the Schedule, such interest to accrue from the date on which the respective amounts are credited to the Reserve Fund.

In the event of termination of this Agreement the Reinsured shall be entitled to retain only sufficient balances to cover the amount of outstanding liability and such balances to be released commensurately with the reduction of this liability until all the obligations of the Reinsurer under this Agreement have been fully discharged.

Article 11: Loss Reserve and Interest

The Reinsured shall also be entitled to retain as at {ANNIVERSARY DATE} of each year an amount equivalent to a percentage, as specified by local legislation, of the outstanding losses in the Reinsured's books as at that date. The outstanding loss reserve so retained shall be released to the Reinsurers as at {ANNIVERSARY DATE} of the succeeding year or years until all outstanding losses for the underwriting year in question have been settled. As at {ANNIVERSARY DATE} of each year the Reinsured shall pay to the Reinsurers interest at the rate specified in the Schedule of the outstanding loss reserve retained during the preceding 12 months.

Article 12: Attachment and Termination

This Agreement takes effect on and from the date specified in the Schedule and applies to all policies written or renewed after that date.

The Agreement is concluded for an indefinite period but may be terminated at that date specified in the Schedule by either party giving three months prior notice in writing by registered letter or telex or cable to the other party. During the term of notice to terminate, and until its expiry, the Reinsured shall renew existing cessions and take new risks in the same manner and in all respects as if no such notice had been given.

Special Cancellation

Either party shall have the right to terminate this Agreement immediately by giving the other party notice:

(a) if the performance of the whole or any part of this Agreement be prohibited or rendered impossible *de jure* or *de facto* in particular and without prejudice to the generality of the preceding words in consequence of any law or regulation which is or shall be in force in any country or territory or if any law or regulation shall prevent directly or indirectly the remittance of any or all or any part of the balance of payments due to or from either party;

(b) if the other party has become insolvent or unable to pay its debts or has lost the whole or any part of its paid up capital;

(c) should the other party reduce its paid-up capital;

(d) should the other party go into liquidation whether voluntary or compulsory or pass a resolution preliminary to liquidation or suffer the appointment of a Receiver;

(e) if there is any material change in ownership or control of the other party;

(f) should the other party amalgamate with or be acquired or controlled by any other company or corporation;

(g) if the other party shall have failed to meet its obligations under this agreement or to comply with any of the terms and conditions of this agreement;

(h) should the other party commit any breach of the conditions of this Agreement;

(i) if the country or territory in which the other party resides or has its head office or is incorporated shall be involved in armed hostilities with any other country whether war be declared or not or is partly or wholly occupied by another power, always providing that the circumstances detailed herein have the effect of rendering the performance of the whole or any part of this Agreement impossible.

All notices of termination in accordance with any of the provisions of this paragraph shall be by the quickest means available and shall be deemed to be served upon despatch or where communications between the parties are interrupted upon attempted despatch. All notices of termination served in accordance with any of the provisions of this Article shall be addressed to the party concerned at its head office or at any other address previously designated by that party.

Should the Agreement be cancelled in accordance with any of the foregoing Special Cancellation provisions, the Reinsured shall at the date of termination cancel the whole of the reinsurance ceded hereunder and the Reinsured shall be entitled to be repaid by the Reinsurers a proportionate part from the date of such cancellation of all premiums paid or credited to the Reinsurers on the cancelled reinsurances in respect of any period extending beyond the date of cancellation. Furthermore the Reinsurer shall remain liable for losses occurring up to and including the date of such termination. Thereafter the liability of the Reinsurer shall cease outright other than as far as outstanding claims are concerned.

Article 13: Errors and Omissions

Any error and/or inadvertent omission in connection with the application of this Agreement shall not prejudice the rights of either party but shall be corrected immediately upon discovery so that the parties hereto shall be placed in the same position as if the error and/or inadvertent omission had not occurred.

Article 14: Confidentiality

The Reinsurers shall regard the transactions under this Agreement as strictly confidential and shall not at any time, during its currency or thereafter, make any use, either directly or indirectly, of the information afforded of the business and connections of the Reinsured which shall or may in any way operate to the prejudice or detriment of the latter.

Article 15: Alterations and Amendments

Any alterations which may from time to time become necessary to this Agreement may be made by addendum or by correspondence, the documents embodying such alterations as may be mutually agreed upon being attached to this Agreement and forming an integral part thereof.

Article 16: Arbitration

All disputes arising out of this Agreement or concerning its interpretations or validity whether arising before of after its termination shall be referred to a Court of Arbitration which shall consist of two Arbitrators who shall be active or retired officials of Companies or underwriters carrying on a similar type of insurance or reinsurance business to that covered hereunder; one to be appointed by each party, and an Umpire who shall be appointed by the Arbitrators immediately after they themselves shall have been appointed and in the event of the Arbitrators being unable to reach agreement on the reference the Umpire shall forthwith enter on the reference in lieu of the Arbitrators.

If either of the appointed Arbitrators for any reason whatsoever fails to act, the party by whom he was appointed shall by writing appoint an Arbitrator in his place and should either party fail to appoint an Arbitrator within one month after being requested by the other party in writing to do so, or in the event of the Arbitrators failing to agree as to the appointment of the Umpire within one month after their own appointment such Arbitrator or Umpire as the case may be shall be appointed in writing by the Secretary General for the time being of the Court of Arbitration of the International Chamber of Commerce at the written request of either party.

The Arbitrators or Umpire as the case may be shall determine any reference in accordance with current reinsurance market practice pertaining during the period of this Agreement and in making their award shall at the same time decide as to the payment of the cost of the arbitration. The Court of Arbitration shall take place in {CITY} and the law applicable to both the aforesaid Agreement and this arbitration agreement shall be the law of {COUNTRY}.

This arbitration agreement shall be construed as a separate and independent contract between the parties hereto and arbitration hereunder shall be a condition precedent to the commencement of any action at law.

Article 17: Intermediary Clause

{NAME OF BROKER} are hereby recognised as the intermediary negotiating this Agreement for all business hereunder. All communications and documents relating hereto shall be transmitted to the Reinsured and the Reinsurers through {NAME AND ADDRESS OF BROKER}

SCHEDULE

Attaching to and forming part of Reinsurance Agreement No. {POLICY NUMBER} for account of

(1) CLASS OF BUSINESS AND TREATY LIMITS: (Article 1) — Applicable to each class

(2) TREATY CESSION: (Article 1) — Up to {NUMBER} Gross Lines of up to a maximum of {AMOUNT} per line any one risk or as specified in the attached schedule. {NOTE: A schedule should be

138 Specimen Treaty Wordings

	attached showing the retentions and treaty limits for each class of business accepted}
(3) **COMMISSION:** (Article 6)	%
(4) **TAXES:** (Article 6)	As per local legislation.
(5) **PROFIT COMMISSION:** (Article 7)	% on the combined results of Fire, Miscellaneous Accident, Renewable Engineering, Contractors All Risks and Erection All Risks Section. % Reinsurers Expenses Deficit to be carried forward for a maximum of {NUMBER} further underwriting years.
(6) **CASH LOSS LIMIT:** (Article 8)	{AMOUNT} for 100% Reinsurers' share.
(7) **ACCOUNTS:** (Article 9)	To be Compiled as at: {DATES} of each year
(8) **MAIN CURRENCY:** (Article 9)	
(9) **PREMIUM RESERVE:** (Article 10)	% as per local legislation subject to interest at % per annum.
(10) **LOSS RESERVE:** (Article 11)	% or as per local legislation subject to interest at % per annum.
(11) **COMMENCEMENT DATE:** (Article 12)	Risks attaching on or after {DATE}.
(12) **NOTICE OF CANCELLATION:** (Article 12)	3 months notice of cancellation to expire on {ANNIVERSARY DATE} In the event of cancellation of this Agreement long term policies will continue to run to their individual anniversary dates.

In witness whereof both the Agreement and Schedule are made in duplicate and signed as under by each of the contracting parties signifying their Agreement to both documents.

For and on behalf of the Reinsured this   day of   , 19

. . . .

and for *REINSURERS* named in the individual Signing Schedules attached hereto. The subscribing reinsurers' obligations under contracts of reinsurance to which they subscribe are several and not joint and are limited solely to the extent of their individual subscriptions. The subscribing reinsurers are not responsible for the subscription of any co-subscribing reinsurer who for any reason does not satisfy all or part of its obligations.

RETENTION TABLE FOR FIRE DEPARTMENT BUSINESS

Maximum percentage of the Gross Lines to be retained per risk category.

Construction/Occupancy	I	II	III
A	100	80	60
B	100	75	50
C	80	60	40
D	60	45	30
E	30	R	R
F	R	R	R

R = Refer to General Manager

Notes

1. Occupancy classification

A. Independent non-hazardous, non-manufacturing risks with no storage of stock-in-trade.
B. Independent non-hazardous commercial and light industrial risks with incidental storage of stock-in-trade/process and with good standard of fire protection.
C. Non-hazardous retail and wholesale commercial risks with no production or manufacturing process.
D. Non-hazardous light industrial risks and workshops.
E. Other non-hazardous risks.
F. Risks with either hazardous storage or process involved.

2. Construction classification

Based on construction of external walls and roof.

I   Reinforced concrete, concrete blocks, bricks, stone and the like.
II Roof of galvanised corrugated iron sheets, aluminium or asbestos on steel/iron frame and brick/concrete block walls.
III Wholly constructed of sheets of galvanised/corrugated iron or aluminium sheets on steel or timber frames and other mixed construction not classified above.

NUCLEAR ENERGY RISKS AS PER THE NUCLEAR ENERGY RISKS EXCLUSION CLAUSE (REINSURANCE) (1994)—NMA 1975A

[*Full wording of this clause appears on page 150*]

MOTOR AND GENERAL LIABILITY EXCESS OF LOSS

REINSURANCE AGREEMENT

made between

———

(hereinafter referred to as the "Reinsured")

of the one part

and

CERTAIN REINSURERS named in the individual Signing Schedules attached hereto. The subscribing reinsurers' obligations under contracts of reinsurance to which they subscribe are several and not joint and are limited solely to the extent of their individual subscriptions. The subscribing reinsurers are not responsible for the subscription of any co-subscribing reinsurer who for any reason does not satisfy all or part of its obligations.

(hereinafter called the "Reinsurers") of the other part.

WHEREBY IT IS AGREED AS FOLLOWS:

Article 1: Term of Agreement

This Agreement shall apply to losses occurring during the period commencing on {DATE} and ending on {DATE}.

Article 2: Territorial Scope

This agreement shall apply to risks written and located in {COUNTRY/IES}, including incidental extensions worldwide.

Article 3: Classes of Policies or Perils Covered

This Agreement shall apply to all policies of insurance and reinsurance written by the Reinsured, subject to the exclusions contained in Appendix covering the following:

- Motor (All Sections including Personal Accident Benefits) including Contractors Plant and Equipment whether in use as tools of trade or otherwise.
- General Third Party Liability
- Workmen's Compensation (including off-duty extensions) and Common Law benefits including Employers Liability as per legislation

in the location of the risks, or per legislation of the country of the labourer or per legislation of the country of hire.
- All Special Acceptances previously agreed to be automatically covered by all reinsurers subject no material alteration.

Article 4: Reinsuring Clause

The Reinsurers hereby agree to indemnify the Reinsured for that part of their ultimate net loss which exceeds the amount stated in the schedule under the heading "EXCESS" in respect of each and every loss with a limit of liability to Reinsurers of the amount stated in the schedule under the heading "LIMIT" ultimate net loss each and every loss.

The term "each and every loss" where used herein shall be understood to mean all individual accidents or occurrences arising out of and directly occasioned by one event.

Article 5: Index Clause

A. In the event of any loss hereunder the retention of the Reinsured and the limit of liability of the Reinsurers shall be adjusted by reference to an index, as hereinafter defined, applying at {DATE} in the manner hereinafter set out. The index at the above mentioned date shall be called the BASE INDEX.

B. In respect of any loss settlement(s) made under this Agreement, the Reinsured shall submit a list of payments comprising such loss settlement(s) showing the amount(s) paid and the date(s) of payment. However all payments (including legal costs) to one victim excluding continuing regular payments, shall be aggregated and the index at the date of payment, as defined below, shall be that applying at the time that the final payment for compensatory damages is made. The amount of each such payment, and/or continuing regular payment, shall be adjusted by means of the following formula:

$$\frac{\text{Amount of Payment} \times \text{Base Index}}{\text{Index at Date of Payment}} = \text{Adjusted Payment Value}$$

All actual payments and adjusted payment values shall be separately totalled, and the retention of the Reinsured, and the limit of liability of the Reinsurers, shall be multiplied by the fraction:

$$\frac{\text{Total of Actual Payment}}{\text{Total of Adjusted Payment Values}}$$

C. *Definitions*

(a) Index

(i) In respect of an award resulting in continuing regular payments, the index or indices to be applied shall be that to which such an award is linked, and for all other payments the index to be applied shall be that for Wages for the territory in which the claim is made as appearing in the statistics published by the International Monetary Fund.

In the event that this publication does not contain a Wages index for the territory concerned, then the index to be applied shall be that for Consumer Prices published by the International Monetary Fund.

If the publication does not contain any indices for the territory concerned, then an alternative publication shall be mutually agreed by the parties hereto.

    (ii) The index at date of payment shall be the latest available, and/or the index at the date of the first continuing regular payment and subsequently as used to adjust.

(b) The date of payment shall be deemed to be as follows:

    (i) Where no award is made by the Courts the actual date upon which settlement is agreed by the Reinsured.
    (ii) The date an award is made by a Court (if no Appeal is made).
    (iii) The date an award is made by the Appeal Court if the case goes to Appeal. However, in the event that the Appeal Court reduces the damages awarded by the Lower Court, other than changes in apportionment of liability then section (ii) above shall apply.
    (iv) The date from which continuing regular payments commence, or in the event that such payments are adjusted, the date from which such adjustment takes effect.

Notwithstanding the above, it is agreed that the provisions of this Article shall apply to Third Party Bodily Injury losses only. For all other payments, the Adjusted Payment Value shall be the amount of the actual payment.

Article 6: Ultimate Net Loss

The term "Ultimate Net Loss" shall mean the sum actually paid by the Reinsured in settlement of losses or liability after making deductions for all recoveries, all salvages and all claims upon other reinsurances other than underlying reinsurances, to include all adjustment expenses arising from the settlement of claims other than the salaries of employees and the office expenses of the Reinsured. All salvages, recoveries or payments recovered or received subsequent to a loss settlement under this Agreement shall be applied as if recovered or received prior to the aforesaid settlement and all necessary adjustments shall be made by the parties hereto. Provided always that nothing in this clause shall be construed to mean that losses under this Agreement are not recoverable until the Reinsured's ultimate net loss has been ascertained.

Article 7: Conditions

This Agreement shall be deemed to be subject to the same terms, clauses and conditions as the original policies and/or contracts as far as they may be applicable hereto and shall pay as may be paid thereon, but subject nevertheless to the terms and conditions of this Agreement.

This Agreement shall furthermore be subject to the provisions of any Special Conditions embodied in the attached Schedule.

Article 8: Net Retained Lines

This Agreement shall only protect that portion of any insurance or reinsurance which the Reinsured, acting in accordance with its established practices retains net for its own account. Reinsurers' liability hereunder shall not be increased due to an error or omission which results in an increase in the Reinsured's normal net retention nor by the Reinsured's failure to reinsure in accordance with its normal practice, nor by the inability of the Reinsured to collect from any other Reinsurers any amounts which may have become due from them, whether such inability arises from the insolvency of such other Reinsurers or otherwise.

Article 9: Premium

The rate of premium payable by the Reinsured to the Reinsurers and all other conditions regarding the computation and/or payment of premium shall be as specified in the attached Schedule.

Article 10: Reinstatement

In the event of any portion of the indemnity given hereunder being exhausted, the amount exhausted shall be automatically reinstated from the time of commencement of any loss occurrence to the expiry of this Agreement without payment of any additional premium. However, in respect of General Third Party Liability losses the Reinsurers' liability shall never be more than {AMOUNT} in all during the term of this Agreement.

Article 11: Extended Expiration Clause

If this Agreement should expire or be terminated whilst an event which may give rise to a loss hereunder is in progress it is understood and agreed that, subject to the other conditions of this Agreement, the Reinsurers hereon shall be liable as if the entire event had occurred prior to the expiration of this Agreement, provided always that no part of that loss occurrence is claimed against any renewal of this Agreement.

Article 12: Acts in Force Clause

The provisions of this Agreement are based on the benefits payable and other terms as provided for in legislation relating to the business protected hereunder in {COUNTRIES} at the effective date of inception of this Agreement. Should any alterations to such benefits or other terms be made subsequently materially affecting the basis of this Agreement, the parties hereto agree to take up for immediate discussion a suitable revision in the terms of the Agreement. Failing agreement on a revision this Agreement shall operate from the effective date of the change of law as if the change had not occurred.

Article 13: Warranties

It is warranted:
{LIST THE WARRANTIES WHICH MAY APPLY}

Article 14: Termination

Either party shall have the right to terminate this Agreement immediately by giving the other party notice by telex or telegram which shall be deemed to be served upon despatch or where communications between the parties are interrupted upon attempted despatch:

(i) If the performance of the whole or any part of this Agreement be prohibited or rendered impossible *de jure* or *de facto* in particular and without prejudice to the generality of the preceding words in consequence of any law or regulation which is or shall be in force in any country or territory or if any law or regulation shall prevent directly or indirectly the remittance of any or all or any part of the balance of payments due to or from either party.

(ii) If the other party has become insolvent or unable to pay its debts or has lost the whole or any part of its paid up capital.

(iii) If there is any material change in the management or control of the other party.

(iv) If the country or territory in which the other party resides or has its head office or is incorporated shall be involved in armed hostilities with any other country whether war be declared or not or is partly or wholly occupied by another power or be in a state of civil war, provided that the circumstances detailed herein render the performance of the whole or any part of this Agreement impossible.

(v) If the other party shall have failed to comply with any of the terms and conditions of this Agreement.

All notices of termination in accordance with any of the provisions of this paragraph shall be by cable, telex or any other means of instantaneous communication and shall be deemed to be served upon despatch or where communications between the parties are interrupted upon attempted despatch.

In the event of this Agreement being terminated at any date other than its normal expiry date then the premium due to the Reinsurers shall be calculated upon the premium income of the Reinsured up to the date of termination or where applicable *pro rata temporis* of the minimum premium.

Article 15: Currency Settlements

All transactions hereunder shall be in the main currency specified in the Schedule.

For the purpose of this Agreement all premiums received and/or claims paid by the Reinsured in currencies other than the main currency shall be converted into such currency at the rates of exchange used by the Reinsured for the purpose of their own accounts, or where there is a specific remittance for a loss settlement at the rates of exchange used in making such remittance.

Article 16: Notification of Claim

The Reinsured undertakes to advise the Reinsurers as soon as possible of any circumstances likely to give rise to a claim hereunder together with any estimate of the Reinsurer's liability and thereafter keep the Reinsurers fully informed of any developments regarding the claim.

Article 17: Loss Settlements

All loss settlements made by the Reinsured, provided same are within the terms of the original policies or so deemed by a court of competent jurisdiction and within the terms of this Agreement, shall be unconditionally binding upon the Reinsurers and amounts falling to the share of the Reinsurers shall be payable by them upon reasonable evidence of the amount payable being given by the Reinsured.

Claims Control

Notwithstanding the above, the course to be adopted by the Reinsured in connection with the defence or settlement of any claim or claims likely to exceed {AMOUNT} to the Reinsured's Net Account shall be determined between the Reinsured and the Leading Reinsurer or its representatives and the Reinsured shall not without the consent of the Leading Reinsurer or its representatives litigate any such claim or claims.

Article 18: Jurisdiction

Notwithstanding anything contained herein to the contrary it is agreed that the indemnity provided herein shall not apply to compensation for damages in respect of judgments delivered or obtained by a court of competent jurisdiction within the United States of America or Canada.

Article 19: Inspection of Records

The Reinsurers may at any time during normal office hours inspect and take copies of such of the Reinsured's records and documents which relate to business covered under this Agreement. It is agreed that the Reinsurer's rights of inspection shall continue as long as either party has a claim against the other arising out of this Agreement.

The Reinsurers shall regard the transactions under this Agreement as strictly confidential and shall not at any time, during its currency or thereafter, make any use, either directly or indirectly, of the information afforded of the business and connections of the Reinsured which shall or may in any way operate to the prejudice or detriment of the latter.

Article 20: Alterations and Amendments

Any alterations which may from time to time become necessary to this Agreement may be made by addendum or by correspondence the documents embodying such alterations as may be mutually agreed upon being attached to this Agreement and forming an integral part thereof.

Article 21: Proper Law and Jurisdiction

The validity construction and performance of this Agreement is to be governed by English Law and Jurisdiction. {OR STATE COUNTRY}

Article 22: Arbitration

All disputes arising out of the above Agreement or concerning its interpretations or validity whether arising before or after its termination shall be referred to a Court of Arbitration which shall consist of two Arbitrators who shall be active or retired officials of Companies or Underwriters carrying on a similar type of insurance or reinsurance business to that covered hereunder; one to be appointed by each party, and an Umpire who shall be appointed by the Arbitrators immediately after they themselves shall have been appointed and in the event of the Arbitrators being unable to reach agreement on the reference the Umpire shall forthwith enter on the reference in lieu of the Arbitrators.

If either of the appointed Arbitrators for any reason whatsoever fails to act, the party by whom he was appointed shall by writing appoint an Arbitrator in his place and if either party fails to appoint an Arbitrator within one month after being requested by the other party in writing to do so, or in the event of the Arbitrators failing to agree as to the appointment of the Umpire within one month after their own appointment such Arbitrators or Umpire as the case may be shall be appointed in writing by the Secretary General for the time being of the Court of Arbitration of the International Chamber of Commerce at the written request of either party.

The Arbitrators or Umpire as the case may be shall determine any reference in accordance with current reinsurance market practice pertaining during the period of this Agreement and in making their award shall at the same time decide as to the payment of the cost of the Arbitration.

The Court of Arbitration shall take place in London, England. {OR STATE CITY AND COUNTRY}

This Arbitration Agreement shall be construed as a separate and independent contract between the parties hereto and Arbitration hereunder shall be a condition precedent to the commencement of any action at law.

Article 23: Intermediaries Clause

{NAME OF BROKER} are hereby recognised as the Intermediary negotiating this Agreement for all business hereunder. All communications and documents relating thereto shall be transmitted to the Reinsured and the Reinsurers through {NAME AND ADDRESS OF BROKER}

SCHEDULE

Attaching to and forming part of Reinsurance Agreement No. {POLICY NUMBER} for account of {NAME OF REINSURED}

EXCESS: (Article 4)	{AMOUNT OF PRIORITY} Ultimate Net Loss each and every loss.
LIMIT: (Article 4)	{AMOUNT OF LIMIT} Ultimate Net Loss each and every loss.
SPECIAL CONDITIONS: (Article 7)	Exclusions: As per the attached list.
PREMIUM: (Article 9)	The rate of premium payable by the Reinsured to the Reinsurers shall be {RATE} % of the Gross Net Premium Income of the Reinsured for the period of this Agreement in respect of the classes of business covered hereunder.

It is understood and agreed that the Minimum and Deposit Premium for this Agreement shall be {AMOUNT} which the Reinsured shall pay to the Reinsurers half yearly in two equal instalments of {AMOUNT} on {DATE} and {DATE}.

As soon as practicable after {EXPIRY DATE} the Reinsured shall submit details of their Gross

Net Premium Income and the premium hereon shall be calculated at the above rate, the Deposit Premium adjusted accordingly subject always to the Minimum Premium of {AMOUNT}.

The term "Gross Net Premium Income" where used in this Agreement is understood to mean gross premiums accounted for during the period hereof less returned premiums, cancellations and premiums paid for reinsurances, recoveries under which inure to the benefit hereof.

MAIN CURRENCY:
(Article 15)

In witness whereof both the Agreement and Schedule are made in duplicate and signed as under by each of the contracting parties signifying their Agreement to both documents.

For and on behalf of the Reinsured this   day of   , 19

....

and for *REINSURERS* named in the individual Signing Schedules attached hereto. The subscribing reinsurers' obligations under contracts of reinsurance to which they subscribe are several and not joint and are limited solely to the extent of their individual subscriptions. The subscribing reinsurers are not responsible for the subscription of any co-subscribing reinsurer who for any reason does not satisfy all or part of its obligations.

APPENDIX

Attaching to and forming part of Reinsurance Agreement No. {POLICY NO} for account of {NAME OF REINSURED}

EXCLUSIONS

This Agreement shall exclude:

- Obligatory reinsurances other than fronting arrangements.
- Excess of Loss reinsurances.
- Nuclear Energy Risks as per Nuclear Energy Risks Exclusion Clause 1994 (NMA 1975A) as attached.
- Seepage and Pollution as per Seepage and Pollution Clause NMA 1685 and NMA 1686 as attached.

- Losses arising directly or indirectly out of war, invasion, acts of foreign enemies, hostilities (whether war be declared or not), Civil War, Rebellion, Revolution, insurrection, military or usurped power or confiscation or nationalisation or requisition or destruction of or damage to property by or under the order of any government or public or local authority.

The Specific Exclusions for each class of business covered hereunder shall be as follows:

Motor

(a) Sports Meetings, races and rallies including any form of competition in motor propelled vehicles.
(b) Vehicles not on *terra firma*.
(c) Loss or destruction of or damage to any property whatsoever or any loss or expense whatsoever resulting or arising therefrom or any consequential loss, or any legal liability of whatsoever nature directly or indirectly caused by or arising from ionising radiation or contamination by radioactivity from any nuclear fuel or from any nuclear waste from the combustion of nuclear fuel.

Workmen's Compensation and Employers' Liability

(a) Manufacture, storage, filling, breaking down of transport for fireworks, ammunition, fuses, cartridges, powder, nitro-glycerine or any explosives or gases and/or air under pressure. (It is understood and agreed however that the breaking down, storage and transport of any of the above substances which is merely incidental to the occupation and/or work and/or trade of the Insured is not excluded from this agreement).
(b) Miners.
(c) Ships and Air Crew. Notwithstanding these exclusions, policies in respect of ships' crews may be covered hereunder for vessels up to 1,500 tons and not exceeding 15 crew members.
(d) Shipbuilding and ship repairing yards unless incidental.
(e) Construction and other work under water, unless incidental to the Insured's occupation or trade.

General Third Party

(a) Operations and Navigation of ships (other than Light Craft, Ferries, or similar small vessels not exceeding 200 tons with a passenger carrying capacity of not more than 50 persons and plying solely in

150 Specimen Treaty Wordings

Inland or Coastal (i.e. within three miles of the coast) waters, docks and stevedoring risks shipbuilding and ship repairs.
(b) Manufacture, storage filling, breaking down of all kinds of explosives including fireworks, ammunition, fuses, cartridges, powder and nitroglycerine.
(c) Underground mining and quarrying where explosives are used.
(d) Tunnels and Subaqueous works unless incidental.
(e) Gas or Electricity undertakings in respect of any liability arising from power cuts and the like.
(f) Dams and Coffer Dams.
(g) All liability in respect of bodily injury or material damage resulting from operations for the exploration extracting refining storage or transport of liquid or gaseous fuels and/or air under pressure in containers although where storage and transport are merely incidental to the occupation or trade of the Insured they may be included under this agreement.
(h) Chemical Industries producing hazardous materials.
(i) Air transport and all liability for airport and firms engaged in air transport or in handling aeroplanes. However, if liability to aircraft and passengers is excluded then such business may be written.
(j) Products liability in respect of:
   1. Aircraft and/or aviation component manufacturers.
   2. Pharmaceutical Manufacturers.
   3. Manufacturers suppliers and/or distributors of (A) Chemicals/Petrochemicals of an explosive toxic or noxious nature (B) fertilisers pesticides fungicides and animal feeds other than where incidental to Insured's main business.
   4. Shipbuilders and ship repairers and manufacturers of machinery and/or components with Marine applications.
(k) All professional indemnity insurances unless incidental.
(l) Motor Third Party Liability.
(m) Exports to the USA and/or Canada, as defined in the Expona 3 Clause as attached.
(n) Products guarantee and recall.

NUCLEAR ENERGY RISKS EXCLUSION CLAUSE (REINSURANCE) (1994) (WORLD-WIDE EXCLUDING USA AND CANADA)—NMA 1975A

This Agreement shall exclude Nuclear Energy Risks whether such risks are written directly and/or by way of reinsurance and/or via Pools and/or Associations.

For all purposes of this Agreement Nuclear Energy Risks shall mean *all first party and/or third party insurances or reinsurances (other than Workers' Compensation and/or Employers' Liability) in respect of*:

Motor and General Liability Excess of Loss

(i) All Property on the site of a nuclear power station.
Nuclear Reactors, reactor buildings and plant and equipment therein on any site other than a nuclear power station.
(ii) All Property, on any site (including but not limited to the sites referred to in (i) above) used or having been used for:
   (a) the generation of nuclear energy; or
   (b) the Production, Use or Storage of Nuclear Material.
(iii) Any other Property eligible for insurance by the relevant Nuclear Insurance Pool and/or Association but only to the extent of the requirements of the local Pool and/or Association.
(iv) The supply of goods and services to any of the sites, described in (i) to (iii) above, unless such insurances or reinsurances shall exclude the perils of irradiation and contamination by Nuclear Material.

Except as undernoted, Nuclear Energy Risks shall not include:

(i) Any insurance or reinsurance in respect of the construction or erection or installation or replacement or repair or maintenance or decommissioning of Property as described in (i) to (iii) above (including contractors' plant and equipment);
(ii) Any Machinery Breakdown or other Engineering insurance or reinsurance not coming within the scope of (i) above;

Provided always that such insurance or reinsurance shall exclude the perils of irradiation and contamination by Nuclear Material.

However, the above exemption shall not extend to:

1. The provision of any insurance or reinsurance whatsoever in respect of:
   (a) Nuclear Material;
   (b) Any Property in the High Radioactivity Zone or Area of any Nuclear Installation as from the introduction of Nuclear Material or—for reactor installations—as from fuel loading or first criticality where so agreed with the relevant local Nuclear Insurance Pool and/or Association.
2. The provision of any insurance or reinsurance for the undernoted perils:
   —Fire, lightning, explosion;
   —Earthquake;
   —Aircraft and other aerial devices or articles dropped therefrom;
   —Irradiation and radioactive contamination;
   —Any other peril insured by the relevant local Nuclear Insurance Pool and/or Association;
   in respect of any other Property not specified in (1) above which directly involves the Production, Use or Storage of Nuclear Material as from the introduction of Nuclear Material into such Property.

Definitions

"Nuclear Material" means:

(i) Nuclear fuel, other than natural uranium and depleted uranium, capable of producing energy by a self-sustaining chain process of nuclear fission outside a Nuclear Reactor, either alone or in combination with some other material; and

(ii) Radioactive Products or Waste.

"Radioactive Products or Waste" means any radioactive material produced in, or any material made radioactive by exposure to the radiation incidental to the production or utilisation of nuclear fuel, but does not include radioisotopes which have reached the final stage of fabrication so as to be usable for any scientific, medical, agricultural, commercial or industrial purpose.

"Nuclear Installation" means:

(i) Any Nuclear Reactor;
(ii) Any factory using nuclear fuel for the production of Nuclear Material, or any factory for the processing of Nuclear Material, including any factory for the reprocessing of irradiated nuclear fuel; and
(iii) Any facility where Nuclear Material is stored, other than storage incidental to the carriage of such material.

"Nuclear Reactor" means any structure containing nuclear fuel in such an arrangement that a self-sustaining chain process of nuclear fission can occur therein without an additional source of neutrons.

"Production, Use or Storage of Nuclear Material" means the production, manufacture, enrichment, conditioning, processing, reprocessing, use, storage, handling and disposal of Nuclear Material.

"Property" shall mean all land, buildings, structures, plant, equipment, vehicles, contents (including but not limited to liquids and gases) and all materials of whatever description whether fixed or not.

"High Radioactivity Zone or Area" means:

(i) For nuclear power stations and Nuclear Reactors, the vessel or structure which immediately contains the core (including its supports and shrouding) and all the contents thereof, the fuel elements, the control rods and the irradiated fuel store; and
(ii) For non-reactor Nuclear Installations, any area where the level of radioactivity requires the provision of a biological shield.

INDUSTRIES, SEEPAGE, POLLUTION AND CONTAMINATION EXCLUSION CLAUSE (NMA 1686)

This Agreement does not cover any liability for:

(1) Personal Injury or Bodily Injury or loss of, damage to or loss of use of property directly or indirectly caused by seepage, pollution or contamination.
(2) The cost of removing, nullifying or cleaning up seeping, polluting or contaminating substances.
(3) Fines, penalties, punitive or exemplary damages.

This Clause shall not extend this Agreement to cover any liability which would not have been covered under this Agreement had this Clause not been attached. The provisions of this Clause are only applicable to risks situated in the United States of America and Canada.

EMPLOYERS' LIABILITY/WORKMEN'S COMPENSATION
DEFINITION OF INDUSTRIAL DISEASE COVER

Should the Reinsured incur liability under policies of Workmen's Compensation and Employers' Liability for Industrial Disease or Physical Impairment which does not arise from a sudden and identifiable accident or event it is understood and agreed that for the purposes of this Agreement:

(1) each employee of an original insured shall be deemed to be a separate loss occurrence giving rise to an event; and
(2) each loss occurrence shall be deemed to have occurred on the date the original insured is advised of the claim following diagnosis of the Industrial Disease or Physical Impairment by a qualified medical practitioner.

Expona 3

PUBLIC AND PRODUCTS LIABILITY
NORTH AMERICAN EXPOSURE ETC. EXCLUSION CLAUSE

This reinsurance shall expressly exclude:

1. Products Liability for an Insured which to the knowledge of the Reinsured at the time of the Reinsured's acceptance exports products to the USA and/or Canada.
2. USA and/or Canada domiciled risks including branches subsidiaries agencies and sales outlets of non-USA/Canadian Insureds.
3. Professional liabilities of whatsoever kind including Directors' and Officers' Errors and Omissions and Medical Malpractice.
4. Assumed reinsurance of whatsoever kind other than facultative reinsurance.
5. Liability arising from loss portfolio transfers of any kind.

6. Public and/or Products Liability policies which do not limit the interpretation of all terms conditions exclusions and limitations to courts domiciled other than within the legal jurisdiction of the USA and/or Canada.
7. Products Liability (whether written as such or as an extension to a public liability policy) whose limit of indemnity does not compromise the Reinsured's maximum liability in all and in the aggregate for any one annual period.

MARINE CARGO AND HULL EXCESS OF LOSS

REINSURANCE CONTRACT

between

———

(hereinafter called the "Reinsured")

and

INSURANCE AND REINSURANCE COMPANIES

as per INDIVIDUAL Signing Schedules attached hereto

(hereinafter called the "Reinsurer")

This reinsurance is to cover the liability of the Reinsured under all policies and/or contracts of insurance and/or reinsurance in respect of all losses howsoever and wheresoever arising anywhere in the world on business written and retained net in the Reinsured's Marine Cargo and Hull Departments, of all insurances and/or co-insurance from all insurance companies and/or agencies and/or concerns in {COUNTRY}, including Strikes, Riots, Civil Commotion and Malicious Damage Risks. Subject, however, to the exclusions mentioned in the Appendix and to the following terms and conditions.

It is warranted that in respect of hull risks that coverage hereunder is limited to vessels of {NATIONALITY} Flag and/or Ownership and/or Management.

Article I: Reinsuring Clause

This reinsurance is only to pay the excess of an Ultimate Net Loss to the Reinsured of {PRIORITY} each and every loss occurrence with a limit of liability to the Reinsurers of {LIMIT} each and every loss as more fully defined in Article VI.

Article II: Extension of Protection Clause

If this reinsurance should expire whilst a loss and/or occurrence and/or catastrophe and/or disaster and/or calamity and/or series of losses and/or occurrences and/or catastrophes and/or disasters and/or calamities arising out of one event is in progress, it is agreed that subject to the other conditions of this reinsurance, the Reinsurers shall pay their proportion of the entire loss or damage, provided that the loss and/or occurrence and/or catastrophe and/or disaster and/or calamity and/or series of losses and/or occurrences and/or catastrophes and/or disasters and/or calamities arising out of one event commenced before the time of expiration of this reinsurance, provided that no part of that loss is claimed against any renewal of this Agreement.

Article III: Period of Reinsurance Clause

This reinsurance covers all losses as herein defined occurring during the period commencing with the {INCEPTION DATE} and ending with the {EXPIRY DATE} both days inclusive, Local Standard Time at the place where the loss occurs.

Article IV: Ultimate Net Loss Clause

The term "Ultimate Net Loss" means the sum which the Reinsured actually pay in settlement of claims and/or suit and/or in satisfaction of judgements, including expenses of litigation and/or all other loss expenses of the Reinsured (except expenses of their offices and salaried employees) after deduction of salvages and/or recoveries, including recoveries under other reinsurances.

All salvages, recoveries or payments recovered or received subsequent to a loss settlement under this reinsurance shall be applied as if recovered or received prior to the aforesaid settlement and all necessary adjustments shall be made by the parties hereto.

Notwithstanding anything to the contrary contained herein it is hereby agreed that nothing in this Clause shall be construed to mean that losses are not recoverable from the Reinsurer until the Ultimate Net Loss to the Reinsured has been determined.

The amount of the Reinsurer's liability in respect of any loss or losses shall not be increased by reason of the inability of the Reinsured to collect from any other Reinsurers, whether specific or general any amounts which may have become due from them whether such inability arises from the insolvency of such other Reinsurers or otherwise. The Reinsured may include in his Ultimate Net Loss his proportion of a "one loss occurrence" as defined in respect of Policies on an aggregate basis such proportion being determined by ascertaining the percentage which such individual loss occurrence bears to the total amount of the aggregate losses involved and applying such percentage to the amount paid, or payable by the Reinsured. Such calculations to be based on the figures available at the time the Reinsured settles the original claim, subject to any subsequent readjustment.

Article V: Run-off Clause

In the event of this reinsurance not being renewed, if requested by the Reinsured prior to expiry of this reinsurance, it is hereby agreed to extend this reinsurance to cover the liability of the Reinsured in respect of losses occurring during the 12-month period immediately following expiry of this reinsurance arising under Policies and/or Contracts written or renewed by the Reinsured prior to expiry of this reinsurance. In the event of the Reinsured exercising this option an Additional Premium to be mutually agreed, shall be payable to the Reinsurer. Notwithstanding anything contained in the foregoing in the event of the Reinsured and the Reinsurer failing to agree on the amount of Additional Premium mentioned above, this reinsurance shall terminate at the end of the period stated in the Reinsuring Clause.

Article VI: Definition of Each and Every Loss

For the purpose of this reinsurance the term "each and every loss" shall be deemed to mean "each and every loss and/or occurrence and/or calamity and/or disaster and/or catastrophe and/or series of any thereof arising out of one event".

Article VII: Net Retained Lines Clause

This reinsurance applies only to that portion of any insurance or reinsurance which the Reinsured retains net for its own account, and in calculating the amount of any loss hereunder and also computing the amount or amounts in excess of which this reinsurance attaches, only loss or losses in respect of any insurance or reinsurance which the Reinsured retains net for its account shall be included.

Article VIII: Premium Clause

The Reinsured shall pay a deposit premium of {AMOUNT} in {NUMBER} equal instalments in advance at {DATES}.

As soon as possible after the expiry of this Agreement the above deposit premium shall be adjusted to an amount equal to a rate of {RATE} % applied to the Reinsured's Gross Net Retained Premium Income as defined below, subject however to a minimum premium of {AMOUNT}. The payment of any adjustment due between the parties shall be made at once.

The term Gross Net Retained Premium Income shall mean the gross premiums accounted for by the Reinsured on business protected hereunder during the period of this Agreement, less only returned premiums and premiums paid for reinsurances recoveries under which inure to the benefit hereof.

Article IX: Reinstatement Clause

In the event of loss or losses occurring under this reinsurance it is hereby mutually agreed to reinstate this reinsurance to its full amount of {LIMIT} from the time of such loss or losses until expiry of this reinsurance. Such reinstatement shall be made subject to an additional premium calculated at 100 per cent of the full annual premium, reduced pro rata in the same proportion that the amount of loss bears to the full limit of this reinsurance.

But nevertheless the Reinsurer shall never be liable for more than {LIMIT} in respect of any one loss, as defined nor for more than {TOTAL AMOUNT OF LIMIT PLUS ALL REINSTATEMENTS} in respect of all losses during the period of this reinsurance.

Such reinstatement shall include any reinstatement of losses sustained by the Reinsured in respect of War Risks which shall be subject of the provisions of the "War Inclusion Clause".

Article X: War Inclusion Clause

(a) This Clause includes loss, damage, liability or expense caused by or resulting from the risks of War as covered in the original policy(ies) provided that such loss, damage, liability or expense would be recoverable under the terms and conditions of the relevant Institute War Clauses or War sections of the relevant Institute War and Strikes Clauses or relevant London aviation clauses in current use at the inception of this reinsurance or at the time when the War risks cover would have commenced under the original insurance within the terms of these clauses, whichever is the earlier, except that if the risks of War are covered in the original policy(ies) under clauses approved by the London Hull War Risks Joint Sub-Committee, or in respect of Cargo interests under the Standard War Risks Clause of any country which complies with the limitations of the United Kingdom Waterborne Agreement, the foregoing proviso shall not apply.

(b) In the event of loss or losses occurring under this section of the Reinsurance (War Inclusion Clause) the reinsurance shall be automatically reinstated to its full amount from the time of such loss or losses until expiry of the reinsurance in accordance with the general reinstatement conditions of the reinsurance. Nevertheless, and irrespective of any other reinstatement conditions of the reinsurance the Reinsurer shall never be liable for more than {LIMIT} in respect of any one loss nor for more than {TWICE THE LIMIT} in respect of all losses coming within this section of the reinsurance and which occur during the period of this reinsurance, subject however to such overall limitation of cover as may be stipulated in the general reinstatement conditions of this reinsurance.

Article XI: Inspection of Records

No further particulars shall be required by the Reinsurer but the books of the Reinsured, so far as they concern the insurances or reinsurances falling within the scope of this reinsurance, shall be open to the inspection of an authorised representative of the Reinsurer at any reasonable time during the continuance of this reinsurance or of any liability hereunder.

Article XII: Amendments and Alterations

It is hereby understood and agreed that any amendments and/or alterations to this reinsurance that are agreed, either by correspondence and/or Broker's Slip endorsements, shall be automatically binding hereon and shall be considered to form an integral part hereof. All amendments and alterations will be promulgated by Addendum as soon as possible.

Article XIII: Currency Settlements Clause

All transactions hereunder shall be in {CURRENCY} and all premiums received or claims paid by the Reinsured in currencies other than {CURRENCY} shall be converted at the rate of exchange as shown in the books of the Reinsured.

Article XIV: Claims Clause

In the event of a claim arising hereunder notice shall be given to the Reinsurer through {NAME OF BROKER}, as soon as practicable, but inadvertent error or omission of such notification shall not prejudice this reinsurance.

All loss settlements made by the Reinsured, shall be binding upon the Reinsurer provided that such settlements are within the terms and conditions of the original policies and within the terms of this reinsurance and amounts falling to the share of the Reinsurer shall be payable by them upon reasonable evidence of the amount paid being given by the Reinsured.

Article XV: Losses Discovered or Claims Made Clause

It is understood and agreed that as regards losses arising under policies and/or contracts covering on a "Losses Discovered" or "Claims Made" basis, that is to say policies and/or contracts in which the date of discovery of the loss or the date when the claim is made determines under which policy or contract the loss is collectible, such losses are covered hereunder irrespective of the date on which the loss occurs provided that the date of the discovery of the loss, in respect of policies and/or contracts on a "Losses Discovered" basis or the date the claim is made, in respect of policies and/or contracts on a "Claims Made" basis, falls within the period of this reinsurance.

For the purpose of the foregoing the date of the first discovery of a loss occurrence or the date a claim is first made, shall be the date applicable to the entire loss and the Reinsurer shall be liable for their proportion of the entire loss irrespective of the expiry date of this reinsurance provided that such data falls within the period of this reinsurance.

Article XVI: Special Cancellation Provisions Clause

(1) Either party shall have the right to terminate this reinsurance immediately by giving the other party notice:

    (a) If the performance of the whole or any part of this reinsurance be prohibited or rendered impossible *de jure* or *de facto* in particular and without prejudice to the generality of the preceding words in consequence of any law or regulation which is or shall be in force in any country or territory or if any law or regulation shall prevent directly or indirectly the remittance of any or all or any part of the balance of payments due to or from either party.
    (b) If the other party has become insolvent or unable to pay its debts or has lost the whole or any part of its paid up capital.
    (c) If there is any material change in the ownership or control of the other party.
    (d) If the country or territory in which the other party resides or has its head office or is incorporated shall be involved in armed hostilities with any other country whether war be declared or not or is partly or wholly occupied by another power.
    (e) If the other party shall have failed to comply with any of the terms and conditions of this Agreement.

All notices of termination in accordance with any of the provisions of this paragraph shall be by Telex or Telegram and shall be deemed to be served upon despatch or where communications between the parties are interrupted upon attempted despatch.

(2) All notices of termination served in accordance with any of the provisions of this Article shall be addressed to the party concerned at its head office or at any other address previously designated by that party.

(3) In the event of this reinsurance being terminated at any date other than that stated in Article III then the premium due to the Reinsurer shall be calculated upon the premium income of the Company up to date of termination or *pro rata temporis* of the annual minimum premium, whichever is the greater. The rights and obligations of both parties to this reinsurance shall remain in full force until the effective date of termination.

Article XVII: Nuclear Energy Risks Exclusion Clause (Marine)—M/26/B

This reinsurance shall exclude Nuclear Energy Risks whether such risks are written directly and/or by way of reinsurance and/or via Pools and/or Associations.

For all purposes of this reinsurance Nuclear Energy Risks shall be defined as

all first party and/or third party insurances (other than Workers' Compensation and/or Employers Liability) in respect of:
- (i) Nuclear reactors and nuclear power stations or plant;
- (ii) Any other premises or facilities whatsoever related to or concerned with:
    - (a) the production of nuclear energy or
    - (b) the production or storage or handling of nuclear fuel or nuclear waste;
- (iii) Any other premises or facilities eligible for insurance by any local Nuclear Pool and/or Association but only to the extent of the requirements of the local Pool and/or Association, it being the intention always that the Reinsurer shall follow the fortunes of the Reinsured insofar as the Reinsured complies with the requirements of any such local Pool and/or Association;
- (iv) Nuclear and/or radioactive fuel or nuclear and/or radioactive waste.

However, this Exclusion shall not apply.

- (a) to any insurance or reinsurance in respect of the construction, erection or installation of buildings, plant and other property (including contractor's plant and equipment used in connection therewith).
    - (i) for the storage of nuclear fuel—prior to the commencement of storage
    - (ii) as regards reactor installations—prior to the commencement of loading of nuclear fuel into the reactor, or prior to the initial criticality, depending on the commencement of the insurance or reinsurance of the relevant local Nuclear Pool and/or Association.
- (b) to any Machinery Breakdown or other Engineering insurance or reinsurance not coming within the scope of (a) above, nor affording coverage in the "high radioactivity" zone;
- (c) to any insurance or reinsurance in respect of the Hulls of ships and/or aircraft and/or conveyances;
- (d) to any insurance or reinsurance in respect of loss of or damage to (including any expenses incurred therewith) nuclear and/or radioactive fuel or nuclear or radioactive waste whilst in transit as cargo.

Article XVIII: Non-Marine Liability Exclusion Clause (1/10/87 Amended) Applicable to Original Policies Attaching Between 1 March 1987 and 31 December 1990)

This reinsurance excludes claims for:

1. products liability, unless written on a "claims made" basis within general liability policies; this exclusion of products liability shall not apply to marine vessels, craft, offshore installations or aircraft;

2. directors' and officers' liability;
3. liability under the Securities Exchange Act;
4. professional indemnity and errors and omissions, unless directly related to:
    - owning or handling ships, cargoes or goods in transit;
    - classification societies or marine surveyors.

Article XIX: Excess Loss Aggregate Voyage Extension Clause (Cargo)

The Reinsured may, if he requires, aggregate cargo losses of the same nature (including liability for such loss or damage, and related expenses including general average contribution, salvage charges and expenses incurred to avert or minimise such loss or damage) and treat them as losses arising out of one event provided that:

— it is not possible to determine the quantum of loss applicable to separate occurrences or events; and
— that such losses are in respect of cargo carried in the same vessel for the same or an overlapping voyage.

The date of loss in such cases shall be deemed to be the date of arrival at the port of discharge of such cargo or the date of discovery of loss if earlier. If such cargo is discharged at more than one port, the date of loss shall be deemed to be the date of arrival at the first port of discharge or the date of discovery of loss if earlier.

Claims paid by the Reinsured in respect of any interests other than cargo as described above are specifically excluded from the protection afforded by this Clause.

The Reinsurer's liability hereunder in respect of any one such aggregate loss is subject to the terms and conditions of this reinsurance, and shall not exceed the limit of indemnity provided herein in respect of each loss.

Article XX: Seepage and Pollution Exclusion Clause (01.01.89) (M/31/D)

This reinsurance excludes any loss arising from seepage, pollution or contamination on land unless such risks are insured solely on a sudden and accidental basis. This contract also excludes liability in respect of disposal or dumping of any waste materials or substances.

These exclusions shall not apply to coverage provided in respect of:

(a) control of well policies where such seepage, pollution or contamination follows a well out of control above the surface of the ground or waterbottom;
(b) liability under:
    (1) Offshore Pollution Liability Agreement;

(2) Outer Continental Shelf Lands Act, Federal Water Quality Improvement Act, Arctic Waters Pollution Protection Act;
(3) Seepage, pollution or contamination covered by Protection and Indemnity policies;
(4) Aviation policies subject to clauses no less restrictive than AVN 46B.

Article XXI:
Institute Radioactive Contamination Exclusion Clause (Cl.356) 01.10.90.

This clause shall be paramount and shall override anything contained in this insurance inconsistent therewith.

(1) In no case shall this insurance cover loss, damage, liability or expense directly or indirectly caused by or contributed to by or arising from:
   (i) ionising radiations from or contamination by radioactivity from any nuclear fuel or from any nuclear waste or from the combustion of nuclear fuel;
   (ii) the radioactive, toxic, explosive or other hazardous or contaminating properties of any nuclear installation, reactor or other nuclear assembly or nuclear component thereof;
   (iii) any weapon of war employing atomic or nuclear fission and/or fusion or other like reaction or radioactive force or matter.

Radioactive Contamination Exclusion Clause (USA Endorsement)

This insurance (reinsurance) is subject to the Institute Radioactive Contamination Exclusion Clause 1/10/90 provided that:

- if fire is an insured peril; and
- where the subject matter insured or, in the case of a reinsurance, the subject matter insured by the original insurance, is within the USA, its islands, onshore territories or possessions; and
- a fire arises directly or indirectly from one or more of the causes detailed in Sub-Clauses 1.1 and 1.2 of the Institute Radioactive Contamination Exclusion Clause 1/10/90;

any loss or damage arising directly from that fire shall, subject to the provisions of this insurance (reinsurance), be covered, EXCLUDING however any loss damage liability or expense caused by nuclear reaction nuclear radiation or radioactive contamination arising directly or indirectly from that fire.

Article XXII: Liability Exclusion Clause "B" 1/12/90 (in respect of risks attaching on or after 1 January 1991)

This reinsurance excludes claims in respect of sums which any original assured becomes liable to pay to any other party, unless arising from those policies underwritten by the original insurer on a "claims made" or "losses discovered" basis, and then only where the original claim, or notification of the event giving rise to the claim, is "made" or loss "discovered" during the period of this contract.

Notwithstanding the foregoing this clause shall not exclude claims arising from:

(1) the ownership, management, operation or chartering of marine or inland waterway vessels, craft or units:
(2) the construction, repair or demolition of marine or inland waterway vessels, craft or units and all related components;
(3) operations in respect of bridges, tunnels, sea walls, marine terminals, ports, harbours, wharves, piers, jetties, docks, berths, pontoons, marinas, fish farms, stevedores, divers, marine agents and boat dealers;
(4) offshore exploration, drilling or production, including all related construction operations;
(5) construction, refurbishment, conversion or demolition, but in respect of onshore risks only where policies contain a discovery or cut-off clause effective no more than 36 months after expiry of the policy and any completed operations cover afforded therein;
(6) the ownership, management or operation of aircraft or airports;
(7) construction of aircraft and all related components;
(8) transit, and storage in the ordinary course of transit, of cargo by sea or air, and by land conveyance other than pipeline;
(9) onshore workers' compensation or employers' liability losses arising from the following perils:
fire, lightning, explosion, structural collapse, windstorm, hail, flood, seismic activity, volcanic eruption, collision, riots, strikes, civil commotion, malicious damage;
(10) any cover for physical loss, damage or consequential loss contingent thereon effected by an original assured on behalf of another party.

Notwithstanding anything contained herein to the contrary, this contract excludes:

- directors' and officers' liability;
- liability under the Securities Exchange Act;
- professional indemnity and errors and omissions, unless directly related to:
owning or handling ships, cargoes or goods in transit; classification societies or marine surveyors.

The reinsurers' liability hereunder is subject to the terms, conditions and exclusions of this contract, and shall not exceed the limit of indemnity provided herein in respect of each loss.

Article XXIII: Collusion Amendment (01.04.89)

The Reinsured may aggregate settlements in respect of loss to any single original assured arising from infidelity or fraud committed by any person acting alone or by persons acting in collusion, whether incurred in respect of:

- claims on original policies; or
- under the terms of any reinsurance.

Such settlements may not be aggregated under this contract if they have been settled:

(a) as separate losses under the original policies; or
(b) under separate original policy years.

Nevertheless settlements defined under (b) shall be admissible for that portion of any loss which is attributable to any one original policy year.

The date of loss shall be determined by treating the loss as arising on the date of first discovery of loss by the original assured.

Article XXIV

All disputes arising out of this reinsurance or concerning its interpretations or validity whether arising before or after its termination shall be referred to a Court of Arbitration which shall consist of two Arbitrators who shall be active or retired officials of Companies or underwriters carrying on a similar type of insurance or reinsurance business to that covered hereunder; one to be appointed by each party, and an Umpire who shall be appointed by the Arbitrators immediately after they themselves shall have been appointed and in the event of the Arbitrators being unable to reach agreement on the reference the Umpire shall forthwith enter on the reference in lieu of the Arbitrators.

If either of the appointed Arbitrators for any reason whatsoever fails to act, the party by whom he was appointed shall by writing appoint an Arbitrator in his place and should either party fail to appoint an arbitrator within one month after being requested by the other party in writing to do so, or in the event of the Arbitrators failing to agree as to the appointment of the Umpire within one month after their own appointment such Arbitrator or Umpire as the case may be shall be appointed in writing by the Secretary General for the time being of the Court of Arbitration of the International Chamber of Commerce at the written request of either party.

The Arbitrators or Umpire as the case may be shall determine any reference in accordance with current reinsurance market practice pertaining during the period of this Agreement and in making their award shall at the same time decide as to the payment of the cost of the arbitration. The Court of Arbitration shall take place in the country in which the head office of the Reinsured party is situated and the law applicable to both the aforesaid Agreement and this arbitration agreement shall be the law of that country.

This arbitration agreement shall be construed as a separate and independent contract between the parties hereto and arbitration hereunder shall be a condition precedent to the commencement of any action at law.

Article XXV: Several Liability Notice (LSW 1001)

The subscribing Reinsurers' obligations under contracts of reinsurance to which they subscribe are several and not joint and are limited solely to the extent of their individual subscriptions. The subscribing Reinsurers are not responsible for the subscription of any co-subscribing Reinsurer who for any reason does not satisfy all or part of its obligations.

Article XXVI: Intermediary Clause

{NAME AND ADDRESS OF BROKER} are recognised as the Broker negotiating this reinsurance through whom all premiums, losses, documents and communications relating thereto shall be transmitted to both parties.

Signed in .... this .... day of .... 19 ....

....

for and on behalf of the Reinsured

....

and for and on behalf of the Reinsurer as per the attached signing schedules.

GENERAL CATASTROPHE EXCESS OF LOSS

CATASTROPHE EXCESS OF LOSS REINSURANCE AGREEMENT

made between

{NAME OF REINSURED}

(hereinafter referred to as the "Reinsured")

of the one part

and

UNDERWRITING MEMBERS OF LLOYD'S and/or
CERTAIN INSURANCE and/or REINSURANCE COMPANIES

named in the individual Signing Schedules attached hereto.

The subscribing reinsurers' obligations under contracts of reinsurance to which they subscribe are several and not joint and are limited solely to the extent of their individual subscriptions.

The subscribing reinsurers are not responsible for the subscription of any co-subscribing reinsurer who for any reason does not satisfy all or part of its obligations.

(hereinafter referred to as the "Reinsurers")

of the other part

Article 1: Period Clause

This reinsurance shall be effective in respect of all loss or losses occurring during the period commencing {INCEPTION DATE} and ending {EXPIRY DATE} both days inclusive, Local Standard Time.

Article 2: Extended Expiration Clause

Reinsurers agree that if this reinsurance should expire whilst a loss to the Reinsured is in progress, then Reinsurers shall be liable as if the whole loss had occurred during the currency of this reinsurance, provided that no part of any loss shall be claimed against any renewal of this reinsurance.

Article 3: Interest Clause

This reinsurance shall apply to all policies and binders of insurance and/or reinsurance written and retained net by the Reinsured in their Fire Department either Direct or by way of facultative reinsurance.

Notwithstanding anything contained herein to the contrary this reinsurance excludes:

(1) Loss or damage occasioned by or through or in consequence directly or indirectly of any of the following occurrences, namely:
   (a) war, invasion, act of foreign enemy, hostilities or warlike operations (whether war be declared or not) civil war;
   (b) mutiny, civil commotion assuming the proportion of or amounting to a popular rising, military rising, insurrection, rebellion, revolution, military or usurped power, or any act of any person or persons acting on behalf of or in connection with any organisation the objects of which are to include the overthrowing or influencing of any *de jure* or *de facto* government by terrorism or by any violent means.

(2) Nuclear Energy Risks as per the *NUCLEAR ENERGY EXCLUSION CLAUSE (Reinsurance) (1994)—NMA 1975a*

This reinsurance shall exclude Nuclear Energy Risks whether such risks are written directly and/or by way of reinsurance and/or via Pools and/or Associations.

For all purposes of this Reinsurance Nuclear Energy Risks shall mean all first party and/or third party insurances or reinsurances (other than Workers' Compensation and Employers' Liability) in respect of:

(i) All Property on the site of a nuclear power station.
   Nuclear Reactors, reactor buildings and plant and equipment therein on any site other than a nuclear power station.

(ii) All Property, on any site (including but not limited to the sites referred to in (i) above) used or having been used for:
   (a) The generation of nuclear energy; or
   (b) The Production, Use or Storage of Nuclear Material.

(iii) Any other Property eligible for insurance by the relevant local Nuclear Insurance Pool and/or Association but only to the extent of the requirements of that local Pool and/or Association.

(iv) The supply of goods and services to any of the sites, described in (i) to (iii) above, unless such insurances or reinsurances shall exclude the perils of irradiation and contamination by Nuclear Material.

Except as undernoted. Nuclear Energy Risks shall not include:

(i) Any insurance or reinsurance in respect of the construction or erection or installation or replacement or repair or maintenance or decommissioning of property as described in (i) and (iii) above (including contractors' plant and equipment);

(ii) Any Machinery Breakdown or other Engineering insurance or reinsurance not coming within the scope of (i) above;

General Catastrophe Excess of Loss   169

Provided always that such insurance or reinsurance shall exclude the perils of irradiation and contamination by Nuclear Material.

However, the above exemption shall not extend to:
(1) The provision of any insurance or reinsurance whatsoever in respect of:
   (a) Nuclear Material;
   (b) Any Property in the High Radioactivity Zone or Area of any Nuclear Installation as from the introduction of Nuclear Material or—for reactor installations—as from fuel loading or first criticality where so agreed with the relevant local Nuclear Insurance Pool and/or Association.
(2) The provision of any insurance or reinsurance for the undernoted perils:
   — Fire, lightning, explosion;
   — Earthquake;
   — Aircraft and other aerial devices or articles dropped therefrom;
   — Any other peril insured by the relevant local Nuclear Insurance Pool and/or Associations;
in respect of any other Property not specified in (1) above which directly involves the Production, Use or Storage of Nuclear Material as from the introduction of Nuclear Material into such Property.

Definitions

"Nuclear material" means:
   (i) Nuclear fuel, other than natural uranium and depleted uranium, capable of producing energy by a self-sustaining chain process of nuclear fission outside a Nuclear Reactor, either alone or in combination with some other material; and
   (ii) Radioactive Products or Waste.
      "Radioactive Products or Waste" means any radioactive material produced in, or any material made radioactive by exposure to the radiation incidental to the production or utilisation of nuclear fuel, but does not include radioisotopes which have reached the final stage of fabrication so as to be usable for any scientific, medical, agricultural, commercial or industrial purpose.

"Nuclear Installation" means:
   (i) Any Nuclear Reactor;
   (ii) Any factory using nuclear fuel for the production of Nuclear Material, or any factory for the processing of Nuclear Material, including any factory for the reprocessing of irradiated nuclear fuel; and
   (iii) Any facility where Nuclear Material is stored, other than storage incidental to the carriage of such material.

"Nuclear Reactor" means any structure containing nuclear fuel in such an arrangement that a self-sustaining chain process of nuclear fission can occur therein without an additional source of neutrons.

"Production, Use or Storage of Nuclear Material" means the production, manufacture, enrichment, conditioning, processing, reprocessing, use, storage, handling and disposal of Nuclear Material.

"Property" shall mean all land, buildings, structure, plant, equipment, vehicles, contents (including but not limited to liquids and gases) and all materials of whatever description whether fixed or not.

"High Radioactivity Zone or Area" means:
  (i) For nuclear power stations and Nuclear Reactors, the vessel or structure which immediately contains the core (including its supports and shrouding) and all the contents thereof, the fuel elements, the control rods and the irradiated fuel store; and
  (ii) For non-reactor Nuclear Installations, any area where the level of radioactivity requires the provision of a biological shield.
(3) Seepage and Pollution risks as per the INDUSTRIES, SEEPAGE, POLLUTION AND CONTAMINATION EXCLUSION CLAUSE.

This reinsurance does not cover any liability for:
  (1) Personal Injury or Bodily Injury or loss of, damage to, or loss of use of property directly or indirectly caused by seepage, pollution or contamination, provided always that this paragraph (1) shall not apply to liability for Personal Injury or Bodily Injury or loss of or physical damage to or destruction of tangible property, or loss of use of such property damaged or destroyed, where such seepage, pollution or contamination is caused by a sudden unintended and unexpected happening during the period of this reinsurance.
  (2) The cost of removing, nullifying or cleaning up seeping, polluting or contaminating substances unless the seepage, pollution or contamination is caused by sudden, unintended and unexpected happening during the period of this reinsurance.
  (3) Fines, penalties, punitive or exemplary damages.

This Clause shall not extend this reinsurance to cover any liability which would not have been covered under this reinsurance had this Clause not been attached.

(4) Excess of Loss reinsurance as per Excess of Loss Exclusion Clause. This reinsurance in no way applies to protect any liability of the Reinsured other than in respect of direct, facultative and domestic retrocession business, as defined in Article 3. Liability in respect of excess of loss reinsurances is excluded from the protection of this reinsurance and cannot be taken into account in arriving at the amount excess of which liability attaches hereto.

(5) All Liability and/or Casualty Business.

Article 4: Territorial Limits Clause

It is hereby understood and agreed that this reinsurance shall apply to losses occurring on risks situated in {COUNTRY} and incidental interests abroad.

Article 5: Excess Loss Clause

The Reinsurers shall only be liable if and when the Ultimate Net Loss sustained by the Reinsured in respect of Interest as defined herein exceeds {PRIORITY} Ultimate Net Loss each and every loss occurrence.

Reinsurers shall thereupon be liable for the amount of the excess thereof in each and every such instance, but their liability under this reinsurance is limited to {LIMIT} Ultimate Net Loss each and every loss occurrence.

However, it is warranted that two or more risks must be involved in the same loss occurrence before recovery can be effected hereunder.

Article 6: Definition of Loss Occurrence Clause

For the purposes of this reinsurance the term "loss occurrence" shall be understood to mean each and every loss and/or series thereof arising out of one event.

However the duration and extent of any one "loss occurrence" so defined shall be limited to:

(a) 72 consecutive hours as regards hurricane, typhoon, windstorm, rainstorm, hailstorm and/or tornado;
(b) 72 consecutive hours as regards earthquake, seaquake, tidal wave and/or volcanic eruption;
(c) 72 consecutive hours and within the limits of one City, Town or Village as regards riots, civil commotions and malicious damage;
(d) 72 consecutive hours as regards any "loss occurrence" which includes individual loss or losses from any of the perils mentioned in (a), (b) and (c) above;
(e) 168 consecutive hours for any "loss occurrence" of whatsoever nature which does not include individual loss or losses from any of the perils mentioned in (a), (b) and (c) above;

and no individual loss from whatever insured peril, which occurs outside these periods or areas, shall be included in that "loss occurrence".

The Reinsured may choose the date and time when any such period of consecutive hours commences and, if any event is of greater duration than the above periods, the Reinsured may divide that event into two or more "loss occurrences" provided that no two periods overlap and provided no period commences earlier than the above stated date and time of the first recorded individual loss affecting this reinsurance in that event.

Article 7: Ultimate Net Loss Clause

The term "Ultimate Net Loss" shall mean the sum actually paid by the Reinsured in respect of any loss occurrence including expenses of litigation, if any, and all other loss expenses of the Reinsured (excluding, however, office expenses and salaries of officials of the Reinsured) but salvages and recoveries, including recoveries from all other reinsurances, other than any underlying reinsurances, shall be first deducted from such loss to arrive at the amount of liability, if any, attaching hereunder.

All salvages, recoveries or payments recovered or received subsequent to any loss settlement hereunder shall be applied as if recovered or received prior to the aforesaid settlement, and all necessary adjustments shall be made by the parties hereto. Nothing in this Article shall be construed to mean that a recovery cannot be made hereunder until the Reinsured's Ultimate Net Loss has been ascertained.

It is understood and agreed that the Reinsured have underlying reinsurances, recoveries under which inure to their sole benefit.

Article 8: Net Retained Lines Clause

This reinsurance applies only to that part of the original policies which the Reinsured retain net for their own account, and in computing the Ultimate Net Loss, only loss or losses in respect of such net retained part of the original policies shall be included.

The amount of Reinsurers' liability in respect of any loss or losses shall not be increased by reason of the inability of the Reinsured to collect from any other Reinsurers whether specific or general, any amounts which may have become due from them whether such inability arises from the insolvency of such other Reinsurers or for any other reason whatsoever.

Article 9: Notification of Loss Clause

The Reinsured undertake to advise the Reinsurers as soon as possible of any circumstances likely to give rise to a claim hereunder.

Article 10: Errors and Omissions Clause

Any inadvertent error or omission on the part of either the Reinsured or the Reinsurers shall not relieve the other party from any liability which would have attached hereunder, provided that such error or omission is rectified as soon as possible after discovery. Nevertheless, nothing contained in this Article shall be held to override specific terms and conditions of this reinsurance, and no liability shall be imposed on the other party greater than would have attached hereunder had such error or omission not occurred.

Article 11: Settlements Clause

Reinsurers shall be bound unconditionally by all loss settlements made by the Reinsured, including compromise settlements, provided such settlements are within the terms and conditions of the original policies and of this reinsurance and amounts falling to the share of the Reinsurers shall be payable by them upon reasonable evidence of the amount paid being given by the Reinsured.

Article 12: Currency Conversion Clause

All transactions hereunder shall be in the main currency specified in the Schedule.

For the purpose of this Agreement all premiums received and/or claims paid by the Reinsured in currencies other than the main currency shall be converted into such currency at the rates of exchange used by the Reinsured for the purpose of their own accounts, or where there is a specific remittance for a loss settlement at the rates of exchange used in making such remittance.

Article 13: Premium Clause

The premium payable to Reinsurers shall be at a rate of {RATE} per cent of the Gross Net Retained Premium Income accounted for by the Reinsured during the period hereof, on Interest as covered hereby, subject to a Minimum and Deposit Premium of {AMOUNT} payable in two equal instalments of {AMOUNT} due on {DATES}.

As soon as practicable after the {EXPIRY DATE} the Reinsured shall submit a statement of their actual Gross Net Retained Premium Income, whereupon the premium paid for this reinsurance shall be adjusted accordingly. Should the premium so computed be more than the Minimum and Deposit Premium stipulated above, the Reinsured undertake to pay the difference but should it be less there will be no return of premium to the Reinsured.

The term "Gross Net Retained Premium Income" shall mean the gross premiums less return premiums, and premiums in respect of reinsurances, recoveries under which inure to the benefit of this reinsurance, in respect of the Reinsured's net retention on Interest covered hereby.

Article 14: Reinstatement Clause

Reinsurers agree that in the event of the whole or any portion of the liability hereunder being exhausted by loss, the amount so exhausted shall be automatically reinstated from the time of occurrence of such loss provided always that Reinsurers' liability hereon shall not exceed {LIMIT} any one loss nor more than {LIMIT PLUS ALL REINSTATEMENTS} in all during the period of this reinsurance, that is to say {NUMBER} full reinstatement(s).

In consideration thereof, the Reinsured shall pay an additional premium computed at 100 per cent of the final premium hereunder for a full loss or pro-rata for a lesser amount reinstated and shall be paid when losses hereunder are settled. If a loss settlement is made prior to the rendering of the Reinsured's statement of Premium Income in accordance with Article 13 hereof, the Reinstatement Premium shall be provisionally computed on the Deposit Premium for this reinsurance.

Article 15: Amendments and Alterations Clause

It is hereby understood and agreed that any amendments and/or alterations to this reinsurance that are mutually agreed either by correspondence and/or Brokers' Slip Endorsements shall be automatically binding hereon and shall be considered as forming an integral part hereof.

Article 16: Inspection

The Reinsurers may at any time during normal office hours inspect and take copies of the Reinsured's records and documents which relate to business covered under this reinsurance. It is agreed that the Reinsurers' right of inspection shall continue as long as either party has a claim against the other arising out of this reinsurance.

Article 17: Termination Clause

Either party shall have the right to terminate this reinsurance immediately by giving the other party notice:

- (a) if the performance of the whole or any part of this reinsurance be prohibited or rendered impossible *de jure* or *de facto* in particular and without prejudice to the generality of the preceding words in consequence of any law or regulation which is or shall be in force in any country or territory or if any law or regulation shall prevent directly or indirectly the remittance of any or all or any part of the balance of payments due to or from either party;
- (b) if the other party has become insolvent or unable to pay its debts or has lost the whole or any part of its paid up capital;
- (c) if there is any material change in the ownership or control of the other party;
- (d) if the country or territory in which the other party resides or has its head office or is incorporated shall be involved in armed hostilities with any other country whether war be declared or not or is partly or wholly occupied by another power;
- (e) if the other party shall have failed to comply with any of the terms and conditions of this reinsurance.

All notices of termination in accordance with any of the provisions of this paragraph shall be by Telex or Telegram and shall be deemed to be served upon despatch or where communications between the parties are interrupted upon attempted despatch.

All notices of termination served in accordance with any of the provisions of this Article shall be addressed to the party concerned at its head office or at any other address previously designated by that party.

In the event of this reinsurance being terminated at any date other than that stated in Article 1 then the premium due to the Reinsurers shall be calculated upon the premium income of the Reinsured up to the date of termination or *pro rata temporis* of the annual minimum premium whichever is the greater. The rights and obligations of both parties to this reinsurance shall remain in full force until the effective date of termination.

Article 18: Intermediaries Clause

{NAME AND ADDRESS OF BROKER} are recognised as the Broker for this reinsurance, through whom all communications and payments relating thereto shall be transmitted to both parties.

Article 19: Arbitration Clause

All matters in difference between the parties in relation to the contract to which this agreement is attached, including formation and validity, and whether arising during or after the period of that contract, shall be referred to an arbitration tribunal in the manner hereinafter set out.

Unless the parties agree upon a single arbitrator within 30 days of one receiving a written request from the other for arbitration, the claimant (the party requesting arbitration) shall appoint his arbitrator and give written notice thereof to the respondent. Within 30 days of receiving such notice the respondent shall appoint his arbitrator and give written notice thereof to the claimant, failing which the claimant may apply to the appointor hereinafter named to nominate an arbitrator on behalf of the respondent.

Before they enter upon a reference the two arbitrators shall appoint a third arbitrator. Should they fail to appoint such a third arbitrator within 30 days of the appointment of the respondent's arbitrator then either of them or either of the parties may apply to the appointor for the appointment of the third arbitrator. The three arbitrators shall decide by majority. If no majority can be reached the verdict of the third arbitrator shall prevail. He shall also act as Chairman of the Tribunal.

Unless the parties otherwise agree the arbitration tribunal shall consist of persons with not less than ten years' experience of insurance or reinsurance.

The arbitration tribunal shall have power to fix all procedural rules for the holding of the arbitration including discretionary power to make orders as to any matters which it may consider proper in the circumstances of the case with regard to pleadings, discovery, inspection of the documents, examination of witnesses and any other matter whatsoever relating to the conduct of the arbitration and may receive and act upon such evidence whether oral or written strictly admissible or not as it shall in its discretion think fit.

The appointor shall be the {TITLE OF APPOINTOR, e.g. The Chairman for the time being of ARIAS} {ARIAS = AIDA Reinsurance and Insurance Arbitration Society} {AIDA = Association Internationale de Droit des Assurances}.

All costs of the arbitration shall be at the discretion of the arbitration tribunal who may direct to any by whom and in what manner they shall be paid.

The seat of the arbitration shall be in {CITY} and the arbitration tribunal shall apply the laws of {COUNTRY} as the proper law of this agreement and of the contract to which this agreement is attached.

The award of the arbitration tribunal shall be in writing and binding upon the parties who covenant to carry out the same. If either of the parties should fail to carry out any award the other may apply for its enforcement to a court of competent jurisdiction in any territory in which the party in default is domiciled or has assets or carries on business.

Signed in {CITY}, this .... day of .... 19 ....

For and on behalf of: The Reinsured

....

and

....

For and on behalf of: The Reinsurers as per the individual Signing Schedules attached. The subscribing reinsurers' obligations under contracts of reinsurance to which they subscribe are several and not joint and are limited solely to the extent of their individual subscriptions. The subscribing reinsurers are not responsible for the subscription of any co-subscribing reinsurer who for any reason does not satisfy all or part of its obligations.

INDEX

Accounts, treaty, 25–26, 31–32
   Non Marine Surplus Treaty, 133–134
Acquisition costs, 6–7, 57
Adjusters' fees, 9, 12, 32
Administration costs, 57
Admitted reinsurers, 29
Agency commission, 6
Aggregates: gross results of portfolio, 59
Alterations and amendments
   Catastrophe Excess of Loss, 174
   Marine Cargo and Hull Excess of Loss, 159
   Motor and General Liability Excess of Loss, 146
   Non Marine Surplus Treaty, 136
Anniversary date, 49, 50
Arbitration
   Catastrophe Excess of Loss, 175–176
   Motor and General Liability Excess of Loss, 146–147
   Non Marine Surplus Treaty, 136–137
   proportional treaty wording, 52–53
Asbestosis, 116
Attachment and termination: Non Marine Surplus Treaty, 135–136

Balance: property reinsurance programme, 58
Book entry, 38
Bordereaux
   Non Marine Surplus Treaty, 131–132
   proportional treaty wording, 53
Broker binders, 13
Brokers
   cash loss refunds, 33–34
   and coinsurance, 5
   commission, 6, 37
Burning Cost
   definition, 86–90
   excess of loss covers, 80
   spreadsheet model, 90–93
Burning Cost Rating, 75, 95
   excess of loss covers, 85–90
      working covers, 86, 89

"Calling", 29
Cancellation
   Catastrophe Excess of Loss Treaty, 174–175
   Motor and General Liability Excess of Loss, 144–145
   Non Marine Surplus Treaty, 135–136
   notice of, 49–50
   special provisions: Marine Cargo and Hull Excess of Loss, 160
Caribbean area, 109
Cash call, 33
Cash loss refunds, 25, 32–34
Cash in Transit covers, 80
Catastrophe cover, 67, 116
   exposure, 77
   retained exposures, 57–58
Catastrophe excess of loss, 81–83, 126
   "Hours Clause", 80–81, 83
Catastrophe excess of loss treaties, 69, 73–75, 167–176
   amendments and alterations clause, 174
   arbitration, 175–176
   currency conversion clause, 173
   definition of loss occurrence clause, 171
   definitions, 169–170
   errors and omissions, 172
   excess loss clause, 171
   extended expiration clause, 167
   inspection, 174
   interest clause, 167–170
   intermediaries clause, 175
   net retained lines clause, 172
   notification of loss clause, 172
   period clause, 167
   premium clause, 173
   reinstatement clause, 173–174
   settlements clause, 173
   termination clause, 174–175
   territorial limits clause, 171
   Ultimate Net Loss Clause, 172
Catastrophe perils, 59
Catastrophe rating, 108–111
   "as if" losses, 110
   First Loss Scale, 110–111
   indexing of claims, 109

Catastrophe rating—*cont.*
  loss cost, 110–111
  model, 111–114
  PML, 109, 110, 111, 113, 114
Catastrophic losses, 2–3, 72, 116
  Personal Accident treaties, 22
Ceding commission, 6, 7, 25, 27, 30
  excess of loss reinsurance, 10–11
  pro-rata reinsurance, 7
Ceding Company
  cash loss refunds, 33, 34
  Ceding Commission, 27
  cessions to treaties, 19, 22–23
  commission, 37
  errors and omissions, 51
  facultative "lineslip", 13
  facultative reinsurance, 6, 7
  interest on reserves, 30
  loss reserves, 29–30
  losses, 32
  premium and loss portfolio transfers, 35
  premium reserves, 28–29
  premiums, 26
  pro-rata reinsurance, 8
  profit commission, 40–42, 46
  Quota Share Treaty, 39
  self-insured obligations, 51
  Surplus Treaties, 15, 16
  tax on premiums, 28
  treaty reinsurance, 13
  treaty reinsurance: financial aspects, 25
  unlimited liability, 116
Cessions: bordereaux, 53
Cessions to treaties, 26
  basis of cession, 19–23
    per bottom basis, 21
    per person basis, 22
    per policy basis, 21
    per vessel basis, 21–22
    PML basis, 20–21
    Top Location and pro-rata basis, 20, 21, 96
Claims
  distribution: practical exercise, 23–24, 119–120
  notification: Motor and General Liability, 145
Claims bordereaux, 53
Claims clause: Marine Cargo and Hull Excess of Loss, 159
Claims settlements: Non Marine Surplus Treaty, 133
"Clean Cut" basis of accounting, 34, 35–36
Clean Cut Treaty, 27, 35
Coinsurance, 5–6
Commission. *See also* Ceding commission; Profit commission
  and facultative reinsurance, 5–7
  property reinsurance programme: spreadsheet, 68–69

Commission—*cont.*
  sliding scale, 27
  unexpired premiums, 37, 38
Confidentiality: Non Marine Surplus Treaty, 136
"Conflagration", 2
Construction, 19, 23, 24, 59, 60
  classification: Non Marine Surplus Treaty, 139
  table of limits, 55–56
Contract limits: excess of loss cover, 83–85
Contract Rate on Line, 108
Contractors' All Risks, 34, 46
Contracts. *See also* Treaty
  and coinsurance, 5–6
  and facultative reinsurance, 5–6
Contribution, 32
Corporation tax, 28
"Costed out", 9
CRESTA organisation, 109
Crop insurance, 75–76
Currency conversion clause: Catastrophe Excess of Loss Treaty, 173
Currency dealings, 3
Currency devaluation, 30
Currency settlements
  Marine Cargo and Hull Excess of Loss, 159
  Motor and General Liability Excess of Loss, 145

Darwin, 115
Definitions
  of Each and Every Loss: Marine Cargo and Hull Excess of Loss, 157
  treaty reinsurance, 27
Deposit Premium, 80, 84. *See also* Minimum and Deposit Premium
Derivatives, 3

"E & O". *See* Errors and omissions
Earthquakes, 2, 109, 115
Employers' Liability, 80, 115, 149, 153
Engineering treaties, 58
Errors and omissions
  Catastrophe Excess of Loss Treaty, 172
  Non Marine Surplus Treaty, 136
  proportional treaty wording, 51
Excess of loss. *See also* Catastrophe excess of loss; Marine Cargo and Hull Excess of Loss; Motor and General Liability; Risk excess of loss; Working excess of loss
  contracts: errors and omissions, 51
  exposure, 57
  facultative reinsurance, 9–12
  treaties, 13, 21, 71
Excess of loss covers, 71–93, 115. *See also* Burning Cost
  financial aspects, 77–85
  loss payments, 77, 80–83
  practical exercise, 81–83, 125–126

Index

Excess of loss covers—*cont.*
  premium. *See under* Premiums
  reinstatement premiums, 77, 83–85, 125
Excess of loss rating, 95–114. *See also*
  Catastrophe rating; Exposure rating
  property risk excess rating model, 98–108
Excess of Loss Ratio Covers (Stop Loss
  Covers), 75–77
Exclusions
  Catastrophe Excess of Loss Treaty, 168–170
  Marine Cargo and Hull Excess of Loss, 160–165
  Motor and General Liability Excess of Loss, 149–154
  Non Marine Surplus Treaty, 130
Expenses
  adjusters' fees, 9, 12, 32
  administration, 57
  excess of loss reinsurance, 12
  of reinsured, 9
  of reinsurers, 41–42, 47
Exposure rating
  differing values, 96
  First Loss Scale, 97, 102
  Poisson Tables/Formula, 98
  reinstatements, 95–96
  risk profile, 96–97, 98
Exposures
  catastrophe, 77
  property reinsurance programme, 57, 58
Extended Expiration Clause
  Catastrophe Excess of Loss Treaty, 167
  excess of loss cover, 81, 83
  Motor and General Liability Excess of Loss, 143
Extension of protection clause: Marine Cargo and Hull Excess of Loss, 155–156

Facultative "lineslip", 13
Facultative Obligatory cover, 14, 17–19, 20, 23–24, 120
Facultative Obligatory Treaty
  property reinsurance programme, 60
  spreadsheet, 66
Facultative reinsurance, 5–12, 13, 71. *See also*
  Excess of loss; Proportional
Filling treaties, 19, 20
Fire
  as catastrophe, 2
  perils, 19, 26
Fire Brigade Charges, 28
Fire business, 30, 139
Fire treaties, 44, 58
First Loss Discounts, 9
First Loss policies, 9–10
First Loss Scale, 10, 11, 114, 127
  catastrophe rating, 109, 110–111
  exposure rating, 97, 102
Flixborough explosion, 21
Floods, 2

"Fluctuation Loading", 111
Full Reinsurance Clause: pro-rata reinsurance, 8–9
Full reinsurance policy: pro-rata reinsurance, 7

General Catastrophe Excess of Loss. *See*
  Catastrophe Excess of Loss
GNPI. *See* Gross Net Premium Income
Governments
  loss reserves, 29, 30
  and premium reserves, 29
Gross Account Risk Profile, 55
Gross Earned Premium, 27
Gross Lines, 19, 20, 23, 61
  Quota Share Treaty, 15–16
  spreadsheet: property reinsurance programme, 61, 63
Gross Net Premium Income (GNPI)
  Burning Cost, 87
  Burning Cost Rating, 95
  Burning Cost spreadsheet, 90, 91–92
  catastrophe rating, 109, 110, 111, 114
  excess of loss cover, 78, 79–80
  excess of loss rating, 104, 108
  stop loss reinsurance, 76
Gross Premiums, 30
Gross results of portfolio, 59
Group Personal Accident policies, 22

"Hours Clause": catastrophe cover, 80–81, 83
Hurricanes, 2, 115
  Hugo, 109
  Tracy, 115

IAD. *See* "Inner Aggregate Deductible"
IBNR (Incurred But Not Reported), 29–30
Incurred losses, 27, 88
Index clause: Motor and General Liability
  Excess of Loss, 141–142
Indexing of claims: catastrophe rating, 109
Industrial disease, 116, 153
"Inner Aggregate Deductible" (IAD): Burning
  Cost spreadsheet, 90–93
Inspection of records
  Catastrophe Excess of Loss Treaty, 174
  Marine Cargo and Hull Excess of Loss, 158–159
  Motor and General Liability Excess of Loss, 146
  Non Marine Surplus Treaty, 131–132
  proportional treaty wording, 51–52, 53
Interest rate swaps, 3
Interest on reserves, 25, 30
"Internal Arrangements" endorsement, 50
"Internal billings", 9

Jurisdiction: Motor and General Liability
  Excess of Loss, 145–146

"Known accumulations", 22

180 Index

Large risks, 2, 5
"Lays off", 3
Legal advisers, 9
Legal fees, 12
Letter of Credit (LOC), 29
Licensed reinsurers, 29
Limits of cover, 77
Limits, table of: property reinsurance programme, 55–56, 58
Line guide, 19
Lines. *See* Gross Lines; Net Lines; Retentions
Liquidation, of insurer, 12
Lloyd's syndicates, 50
Lloyd's underwriters, 1, 28
Loaded Burning Cost, 86
Location, 19
London Market
  cash loss refunds, 33, 34
  notice of cancellation, 50
Loss adjusters, 9, 32
Loss payments: excess of loss covers, 77, 80–83
Loss portfolio incoming, 25
Loss portfolio withdrawal, 26
Loss ratio, 27, 28. *See also* Stop Loss Covers
Loss reserve and interest: Non Marine Surplus Treaty, 134
Loss reserves, 25, 26, 29–30, 31–32, 40
Loss settlements: Motor and General Liability Excess of Loss, 145
Losses, 32. *See also* PML
  Gross Results of Portfolio, 59
  property reinsurance programme: spreadsheet, 68
Losses discovered/claims made clause: Marine Cargo and Hull Excess of Loss, 159
Lotus 1-2-3, 61, 62, 98, 113, 125

M & D. *See* Minimum and Deposit Premium
Management expenses, 47
Marine Cargo and Hull Excess of Loss
  amendments and alterations, 159
  claims clause, 159
  collusion amendment, 165
  currency settlements clause, 159
  definition of Each and Every Loss, 157
  excess loss aggregate voyage extension (cargo), 162
  extension of protection clause, 155–156
  inspection of records, 158–159
  intermediary clause, 166
  liability exclusion clause, 164–165
  losses discovered/claims made clause, 159
  net retained lines clause, 157
  non-marine liability exclusion clause, 161–162
  nuclear risks exclusion, 160–161, 163
  period of reinsurance clause, 156
  premium clause, 157
  reinstatement clause, 157–158

Marine Cargo and Hull Excess of Loss—*cont.*
  reinsuring clause, 155
  run-off clause, 156–157
  seepage and pollution exclusion clause, 162–163
  several liability notice, 166
  special cancellation provisions clause, 160
  Ultimate Net Loss Clause, 156
  war inclusion clause, 158
Marine Cargo treaties, 21
Marine Hull treaties, 21–22
Marine markets, 50
Market evolution, 115–116
Marketability: property reinsurance programme, 58
Mexico City, 116
Microsoft Excel, 98, 125
Minimum and Deposit Premium (M & D)
  Burning Cost, 87
  Burning Cost spreadsheet, 90, 91–92
  excess of loss covers, 78–79
Motor business, 13
  insurance: unlimited liability, 83
  reinsurance: excess of loss cover, 85–86, 89
Motor and General Liability Excess of Loss
  Acts in Force Clause, 144
  alterations and amendments, 146
  arbitration, 146–147
  classes of policies/perils covered, 140–141
  conditions, 143
  currency settlements, 145
  definitions, 152
  exclusions, 149–154
  Extended Expiration Clause, 143
  index clause, 141–142
  inspection of records, 146
  intermediary clause, 147–149
  jurisdiction, 145–146
  loss settlements, 145
  net retained lines, 143
  notification of claim, 145
  premium, 143
  reinstatement, 143
  reinsuring clause, 141
  termination, 144–145
  territorial scope, 140
  Ultimate Net Loss, 142
  warranties, 144
Multiple perils/catastrophe zones, 111

NCAD (Notice of Cancellation at Anniversary Date), 50
Net Lines, 16, 20, 23
  spreadsheet: property reinsurance programme, 61, 63
Net retained lines
  Catastrophe Excess of Loss Treaty, 172
  Marine Cargo and Hull Excess of Loss, 157
  Motor and General Liability Excess of Loss, 143

Net underwriting profit, 7
Non Marine Surplus Treaty, 129–139
  accounts, 133–134
  alterations and amendments, 136
  arbitration, 136–137
  attachment and termination, 135–136
  Bordereaux/Inspection of Records, 131–132
  claims settlements, 133
  confidentiality, 136
  errors and omissions, 136
  exclusions, 130
  intermediary clause, 137–138
  loss reserve and interest, 134
  premium, 132
  premium reserve and interest, 134
  profit commission, 132–133
  Registers of Risks, 131
  retention table: fire department business, 139
Non-marine liability exclusion: Marine Cargo and Hull Excess of Loss, 161–162
Non-marine markets, 50
Non-proportional reinsurance. *See* Excess of loss
North America: exclusion clause, 153–154
North Sea oil rigs, 80, 115
Notice of cancellation, 49–50
Notification of claim: Motor and General Liability Excess of Loss, 145
Notification of loss clause: Catastrophe Excess of Loss Treaty, 172
Nuclear risks: exclusions, 139, 150–151, 160–161–163, 168–170

Occupancy, 23, 24, 59, 60
  classification: Non Marine Surplus Treaty, 139
  table of limits, 55, 56
Oil rig explosion: Piper Alpha, 115
"Overriding commission", 7

Pareto Curves, 108–109
"Penal" M & D: excess of loss covers, 79
Pensions, 80
Per bottom basis, 21
Per person basis, 22
Per policy basis, 21
Per risk excess of loss, 57, 82, 83, 96–97, 115, 125
Per vessel basis, 21–22
Period clause
  Catastrophe Excess of Loss Treaty, 167
  Marine Cargo and Hull Excess of Loss, 156
Period and termination: proportional treaty wording, 49–50
Personal Accident protection, 80
Personal Accident treaties, 22
Piper Alpha oil rig explosion, 115
PML (Probable Maximum Loss), 20–21, 58
  catastrophe rating, 109, 110, 111, 113, 114

Poisson Tables/Formula: exposure rating, 98, 104–107
Pollution exclusion clauses
  Catastrophe Excess of Loss Treaty, 170
  Marine Cargo and Hull Excess of Loss, 162–163
  Motor and General Liability Excess of Loss Treaty, 152–153
Portfolio, 2
Portfolio entry, 38
Portfolio transfers, 35, 39, 40
Portfolio withdrawals, 38, 42
Practical exercises
  distribution of premiums, 23–24, 119–120
  excess of loss programme, 81–83, 125–126
  profit commission calculations, 43, 121–123
Premium and loss portfolio transfers, 34–36
Premium portfolio incoming, 25
Premium portfolio transfers, 37, 38
Premium portfolio withdrawal, 26, 37
Premium reserve and interest: Non Marine Surplus Treaty, 134
Premium reserves, 25, 26, 28–29, 30, 31, 40
Premium Trust Funds, 28
Premiums, 26–28. *See also* Burning Cost; Gross Net Premium Income (GNPI); Reinstatement premiums; Unexpired premiums
  catastrophe excess of loss treaties, 173
  distribution: practical exercise, 23–24, 119–120
  excess of loss covers, 11–12, 77–80
    Minimum and Deposit Premium (M & D), 78–79
    other variables, 80
    "penal" M & D, 79
    premium income, 78
    rate, 77–78
    worked example, 79–80
  Gross Earned Premium, 27
  Gross Premiums, 30
  Gross results of portfolio, 59
  Marine Cargo and Hull Excess of Loss, 157
  Motor and General Liability Excess of Loss, 143
  Non Marine Surplus Treaty, 132
  pro-rata reinsurance, 7
  property reinsurance programme: spreadsheet, 68
  property risk excess rating model, 98–99
  tax, 7, 26, 28, 38
  treaty account statement, 25–26
Pro-rata. *See* Proportional
Profile of protected account, 77
"Profile" of risks. *See* Risk profile
Profiles, 58
Profit, of reinsured, 56–57
Profit commission, 17, 26, 40–47
  calculations: practical exercises, 43, 121–123
  deficit carried forward, 43

182 Index

Profit commission—*cont.*
  Non Marine Surplus Treaty, 132–133
  property reinsurance programme, 57
  Quota Share Treaty: retention changes, 46
  shares of individual reinsurers, 46–47
  terminology, 47
  underwriting year basis, 44–46
Property First Loss Rates, 127
Property insurance, 1–3
Property per risk excess of loss, 96
Property Quota Share Treaty, 14–15
Property reinsurance programme, designing
  apportionment over treaty programme, 60–61
  catastrophe, 57–58
  data, 58–60
  exposure, 57, 58
  marketability, 58
  retention, 55, 56
  spreadsheet, 61–69
  table of limits, 55–56
Property risk excess rating model, 98–108
Proportional facultative reinsurance, 7–9
Proportional reinsurance, 71, 115–116
  exposure, 57
  practical exercise: premium distribution, 23–24, 119–120
Proportional treaties, 13, 14–22. *See also* Facultative Obligatory; Quota Share Treaties; Surplus Treaties; Treaty wordings
Provisional notice of cancellation (PNOC), 49–50
Public and Products Liability: North America, 153–154
Pure Burning Cost, 86
Pure risk premium, 10, 11, 113, 114

Quota Share Treaties, 16, 17, 18, 19, 20, 24
  excess of loss covers, 71
  profit commission, 46
  property reinsurance, 14–15, 60–61
  retention, 23, 39
  spreadsheet, 61, 63, 67, 69

Rate: excess of loss premiums, 77–78
Rate on Line: excess of loss cover, 77, 79, 80, 84, 85
Register of cessions, 26
Registers of Risks: Non Marine Surplus Treaty, 131
Reinstatement
  Catastrophe Excess of Loss Treaty, 173–174
  Marine Cargo and Hull Excess of Loss, 157–158
  Motor and General Liability Excess of Loss, 143
  per-risk excess of loss, 115

Reinstatement premiums
  excess of loss covers, 77, 83–85, 125
  exposure rating, 95–96
Reinsurance, 1–3. *See also* Facultative reinsurance; Treaty reinsurance
  market evolution, 115–116
"Reinsured", 13. *See also* Ceding Company
Reserves. *See also* Interest on reserves; Loss reserve(s); Premium reserve(s)
  accounting, 31–32
Retentions, 8, 15, 19, 39. *See also* Gross Lines; Net Lines
  levels of, 26
  property reinsurance programme, 55, 56
  table of, 23, 119–120, 139
Retrocessions, 78
Risk excess of loss programme, 82
Risk excess of loss rating model, 98–108, 111
Risk excess of loss treaties, 71–72, 74, 75
Risk profile
  exposure rating, 96–97, 98
  Gross Account Risk Profile, 55
"Risk transfer" (reinsurance), 3
Run-off clause: Marine Cargo and Hull Excess of Loss, 156–157

Salvage, 26, 32
Self-insured obligations, 51
Settlements clause: Catastrophe Excess of Loss Treaty, 173
Sliding scale commission, 27
Slip policy: pro-rata reinsurance, 7
Slips
  coinsurance, 5
  excess of loss facultative reinsurance, 11
  Facultative Obligatory cover, 18–19
  pro-rata reinsurance, 7–8
  Surplus Treaty, 16–17
Spreadsheets
  Burning Cost model, 90–93
  catastrophe rating model, 111
  excess of loss claims allocations, 125
  property reinsurance programme, 61–69
  property risk excess rating model, 98–108
"Stabilising results", 3
Stop Loss Covers (Excess of Loss Ratio Covers), 75–77
Subrogation, 26, 32
Sum Insured Treaty, 20
Surplus Treaties, 14, 15–18, 20, 23, 24. *See also* Non Marine Surplus Treaty
  property reinsurance programme, 60
  spreadsheet, 61, 63, 64–65, 67, 69

Table of limits: property reinsurance programme, 55–56, 58
Table of Retentions, 23, 119–120, 139
Tax
  on premiums, 7, 26, 28
  unexpired premiums, 38

Index   183

Termination. *See* Cancellation
Territorial limits clause: Catastrophe Excess of Loss Treaty, 171
Territorial scope: Motor and General Liability Excess of Loss, 140
Third Party exclusions, 149–150
Top Location and pro-rata basis, 20, 21, 96
Trans-shipment, 21
Treaty accounts, 25–26, 31–32
Treaty reinsurance, 13–24. *See also* Cessions to treaties; Excess of loss; Facultative Obligatory; Quota Share Treaties; Surplus Treaties; Treaty wordings
   financial aspects, 25–47. *See also* Profit commission; Unexpired premiums
   cash loss refunds, 25, 32–34
   Ceding Commission, 26, 27
   definitions, 27
   interest on reserves, 25, 30
   loss portfolio incoming, 25
   loss portfolio withdrawal, 26
   loss reserves, 25, 26, 29–30, 31–32
   losses, 32
   paid claims, 26
   premium and loss portfolio transfers, 34–36
   premium portfolio incoming, 25
   premium portfolio withdrawal, 26
   premium reserves, 25, 26, 28–29, 30, 31
   premiums, 25, 26
   tax on premiums, 26, 28
   treaty cancellation, 40
   treaty limits, 39–40
  pro-rata treaties, 13, 14–22
Treaty wordings. *See also* Catastrophe Excess of Loss treaties; Marine Cargo and Hull Excess of Loss; Motor and General Liability Excess of Loss; Non Marine Surplus Treaty

Treaty wordings—*cont.*
  proportional
   arbitration, 52–53
   bordereaux, 53
   errors and omissions, 51
   inspection of records, 51–52, 53
   period and termination, 49–50
   self-insured obligations, 51
"Two Risk Warranty": catastrophe covers, 74

Ultimate Net Loss, 11, 12
  catastrophe excess of loss, 73, 172
  excess of loss claims, 125, 126
  excess of loss reinsurance, 72, 74
  loss payments: excess of loss covers, 80
  Marine Cargo and Hull Excess of Loss, 156
  Motor and General Liability Excess of Loss, 142
Underwriters, and coinsurance, 5
Underwriting year basis, 27, 34–35, 44–46
Unexpired premiums, calculation of, 36–47
  See also Profit commission
  1/8ths system, 38, 39
  1/24ths system, 37, 39
  a fixed percentage, 38–40
Unlimited liability, 115, 116
Unlimited Rate on Line, Poisson, 98, 104, 106, 107
Unlimited reinstatements, 115
US dollars, 30

War inclusion clause: Marine Cargo and Hull Excess of Loss, 158
Water damage, 2
Weather, 2, 109, 115
Whole underwriting year, 37
Working covers: Burning Cost rating, 86, 89
Working excess of loss covers, 75, 80
Workmen's Compensation, 149, 153
"Writing a line", 7